QUESTION
OF THE DAY

WHERE
TRUTH
IS THE
DARE

WD

WRITER'S DIGEST
BOOKS

WritersDigest*.com*
Cincinnati, Ohio

Previously published by Sporkfly Media, 2007.

For more resources for writers, visit www.writersdigest.com/books.

To receive a free weekly e-mail newsletter delivering tips and updates about writing and about Writer's Digest products, register directly at www.writersdigest.com/enews.

15 14 13 12 11   5 4 3 2 1

Distributed in Canada by Fraser Direct
100 Armstrong Avenue
Georgetown, Ontario, Canada L7G 5S4
Tel: (905) 877-4411

Distributed in the U.K. and Europe by F&W Media International, LTD
Brunel House, Forde Close, Newton Abbot, Devon, TQ12 4PU, UK
Tel: (+44) 1626-323200, Fax: (+44) 1626-323319
E-mail: enquiries@fwmedia.com

Distributed in Australia by Capricorn Link
P.O. Box 704, Windsor, NSW 2756 Australia
Tel: (02) 4577-3555

Edited by Scott Francis
Designed by Claudean Wheeler & Terri Woesner
Cover illustration by Fotolia.com/Petr Vaclavek
Production coordinated by Debbie Thomas

Thank You

to

Before there was a book, *Question of the Day* was nurtured along by Aubrey Beale, Courtney Schaudel, Andrea Schmidt, Jackie Caputo, Megan Zuena, Nicole Figueiredo, Mike Mira, Johanna Decal and Victoria Lilli. They helped *Question of the Day* come to life by daring to be honest and revealing.

Rafaela Fernandez suggested I turn *Question of the Day* into a book. Jason Barje suggested I turn it into an iPhone app. Without them, you would not be reading this right now.

Paul Newman helped me find Daniel Williams, who built the app. Huge thanks to both of them.

Jane Friedman has provided me with acknowledgement and encouragement beyond what I could ever ask for. The first question of this book certainly applies to her.

Additional thanks to Stephanie Ciani, Rudy Waldner, Susan Bachner, Anne Benkovitz, Michael Tedesco, Lillie Klein, Emily Briggs, Samantha Santiago and Luana Halili for endless support, inspiration, and for asking me the right questions at the right time.

Credits

1 © Fotolia.com/patrimonio designs; 2 © Fotolia.com/Joggie Botma; 3 © iStockphoto.com/blackred; 4 © Fotolia.com/raven ; 5 © iStockphoto.com/LuisB; 6 © iStockphoto.com/jpal999; 7 © Fotolia.com/Olaru Radian; 8 © iStockphoto.com/chuwy; 9 © Fotolia.com/Lizard; 10 © Fotolia.com/Konstantin Sutyagin; 11 © iStockphoto.com/danleap; 12 © Fotolia.com/Rob Pitman; 13 © Fotolia.com/antipathique; 14 © Claudean Wheelr; 15 © Fotolia.com/mustgo; 16 © Fotolia.com/Vjom; 17 © Fotolia.com/Jagoush; 18 © Fotolia.com/Faber Visum; 19 © Fotolia.com/Faber Visum; 20 © DanielBellon/Klaus Bellon; 21 © Fotolia.com/V. Yakobchuk; 22 © Fotolia.com/rook76; 23 © Fotolia.com/Daniel Raja; 24 © Fotolia.com/Wong Sze Fei; 25 © Fotolia.com/Kim D. French; 26 © iStockphoto.com/eb75; 27 © Fotolia.com/Filipebvarela; 28 © iStockphoto.com/Ceneri; 29 © Fotolia.com/gunnar3000; 30 © iStockphotos.com/PeskyMonkey; 31 © iStockphotos.com/wragg; 32 © Folotlia.com/Adam Tomasik; 33 © iStockphoto.com/JulieWeiss; 34 © Fotolia.com/Beboy; 35 © Fotolia.com/Juan Fuertes; 36 © Fotolia.com/Greg Epperson; 37 © Fotolia.com/Olivier Le Moal; 38 © Fotolia.com/Abdul Qaiyoom; 39 © Fotolia.com/Roman Sigaev; 40 © Fotolia.com/Steven Pepple; 41 © Fotolia.com/Steven Pepple; 42 © iStockphoto.com/CreativeArchetype; 43 © iStockphoto.com/Kabby; 44 © iStockphoto.com/adventtr; 45 © Fotolia.com/nsphotography; 46 © Fotolia.com/allirg; 47 © iStockphoto.com/emm4; 48 © Fotolia.com/Yves Damin; 49 © Fotolia.com/ktsdesign; 50 © Fotolia.com/iofoto; 51 © iStockphoto.com/eb75; 52 © Fotolia.com/Yuri Arcurs; 53 © Fotolia.com/BCDesigns; 54 © Fotolia.com/Mikhail Mishchenko; 55 © Fotolia.com/raven; 56 © Fotolia.com/Spiderstock; 57 © Fotolia.com/Jiri Hera; 58 © Fotolia.com/Yuri Arcurs; 59 © Fotolia.com/ann triling; 60 © iStockphoto.com/alashi; 61 © Fotolia.com/psd photography; 62 © iStockphoto.com/aleksandarvelasevic; 63 © Fotolia.com/maigi; 64 © Fotolia.com/artticnew; 65 © Fotolia.com/sumnersgraphicsinc; 66 © Fotolia.com/Gary Blakeley; 67 © Fotolia.com/Laurent Renault; 68 © iStockphoto.com/Storman; 69 © iStockphoto.com/michellegibson; 70 © Fotolia.com/George Mayer; 71 © Fotolia.com/Maksim Pasko; 72 © Fotolia.com/mcsdwarken; 73 © Fotolia.com/drilling in the dark; 74 © Fotolia.com/Login; 75 © Fotolia.com/Login; 76 © iStockphoto.com/Choreograph; 77 © iStockphoto.com/~prokhorov~prokhorov~; 78 © Fotolia.com/rgb; 79 © Fotolia.com/Serhad; 80 © Fotolia.com/CDH_Design; 81 © Fotolia.com/Florin Capilnean; 82 © Fotolia.com/ann triling; 83 © Fotolia.com/Benjamin Haas; 84 © Fotolia.com/Irina Savrasova; 85 © Fotolia.com/Sirena Designs; 86 © Claudean Wheeler; 87 © iStockphoto.com/sdominick; 88 © iStockphoto.com/eb75; 89 © Fotolia.com/Grigory Iofin; 90 © Fotolia.com/Pavel Losevsky; 91 © Fotolia.com/Losswen; 92 © Folotlia.com/Kheng Guan Toh; 93 © Folotlia.com/Kheng Guan Toh; 94 © Fotolia.com/ultramarin; 95 © Fotolia.com/Vasilius; 96 © Fotolia.com/msw; 97 © Fotolia.com/abdulsatarid; 98 © Fotolia.com/Franck Boston; 99 © Fotolia.com/Dmitri Mlkitenko; 100 © Fotolia.com/Dan; 101 © Fotolia.com/Aliaksandr Zabudzko; 102 © Fotolia.com/Christian Pedant; 103 © Fotolia.com/Wollwerth Imagery; 104 © Fotolia.com/WONG SZE FEI; 105 © Fotolia.com/Tetiana Zbrodko; 106 © Fotolia.com/Andrey Armyagov; 107 © Fotolia.com/Andrejs Pidjass; 108 © Fotolia.com/DrHitch; 109 © Fotolia.com/Filipebvarela; 110 © Fotolia.com/detailblick; 111 © Fotolia.com/TheSupe87; 112 © Fotolia.com/Caz; 113 © Fotolia.com/Marc Dietrich; 114 © Fotolia.com/radoma; 115 © Fotolia.com/jwblinn; 116 © Fotolia.com/James Steidl; 117 © Fotolia.com/uoman; 118 © Fotolia.com/uchar; 119 © iStockphoto.com/chuwy; 120 © Fotolia.com/DouDou; 121 © Fotolia.com/TheSupe87; 122 © Fotolia.com/Kundra; 123 © Fotolia.com/Paul Hakimata; 124 © Fotolia.com/JB; 125 © Fotolia.com/Vanessa; 126 © Fotolia.com/endostock; 127 © Fotolia.com/More Images; 128 © Fotolia.com/scusi; 129 © Fotolia.com/Volant; 130 © Fotolia.com/artida; 131 © Fotolia.com/SSilver; 132 © Fotolia.com/Olivier Le Moal; 133 © Fotolia.com/sumnersgraphicsinc; 134 © Fotolia.com/diego cervo; 135 © Fotolia.com/Sergey Kandakov; 136 © Fotolia.com/Valua Vitaly; 137 © Fotolia.com/frankoppermann; 138 © Fotolia.com/Ivan Kruk; 139 © Fotolia.com/Yurok Aleksandrovich; 140 © Fotolia.com/Danussa; 141 © Fotolia.com/Miqul; 142 © Fotolia.com/Ghost; 143 © Fotolia.com/kentoh; 144 © Fotolia.com/Andrzej Tokarski; 145 © Fotolia.com/pandore; 146 © Fotolia.com/Real Illusion; 147 © Fotolia.com/frenta; 148 © Fotolia.com/Christos Georghiou; 149 © Fotolia.com/Christos Georghiou; 150 © Fotolia.com/seasonal art; 151 © Fotolia.com/Beth Van Trees; 152 © Fotolia.com/Maksim Samasiuk; 153 © Fotolia.com/icholakov; 154 © Fotolia.com/screenexa; 154 © Fotolia.com/rolffimages; 155 © Fotolia.com/aalto; 156 © iStockphoto.com/sylvanworks; 157 © iStockphoto.com/Palto; 158 © iStockphotos.com/spxChrome; 159 © iStockphotos.com/kjohansenkjohansen; 160 © Fotolia.com/M. Dykstra; 161 © Fotolia.com/Adrian Hillman; 162 © Fotolia.com/icholakov; 163 © iStockphoto.com traffic_analyzer163; 164 © iStockphoto.com/Nadzeya Kizilava; 165 © iStockphoto.com/BeholdingEye; 166 © iStockphoto.com/greg801; 167 © iStockphoto.com/bodhihill; 168 © Fotolia.com/ahhuwenjun; 169 © Fotolia.com/OMKAR A.V; 170 © Fotolia.com/laxmi; 171 © Fotolia.com/rudall30; 172 © iStockphotos.com/Mist; 173 © Fotolia.com/lynea; 174 © Fotolia.com/ahhuwenjun; 175 © Fotolia.com/iofoto; 176 © iStockphoto.com/arenacreative; 177 © Fotolia.com/AlterYourReality; 178 © iStockphoto.com/Ed-blitzkrieg; 179 © iStockphoto.com/Janis Lacis; 180 © Fotolia.com/tiero; 181 © Fotolia.com/vlorzor; 182 © Fotolia.com/kathy libby; 183 © fotolia.com/meschke; 184 © Fotolia.com/ahhuwenjun; 185 © Fotolia.com/Acik; 186 © Fotolia.com/Nimbus; 187 © Fotolia.com/gunnar3000; 188 © Fotolia.com/Dragan Boskovic; 189 © Fotolia.com/electricyew; 190 © Fotolia.com/MORO; 191 © iStockphoto.com/chuwy; 192 © iStockphoto.com/milmirko; 193 © Fotolia.com James Steidl; 194 © Fotolia.com/Mike Kiev; 195 © Fotolia.com/Andrei; 196 © Fotolia.com/Terry Morris; 197 © Fotolia.com/Martin Cintula; 198 © Fotolia.com/dorisblick; 199 © Fotolia.com/Barry Barnes; 200 © Fotolia.com/hibridal3; 201 © Fotolia.com/Helder Almeida; 202 © Fotolia.com/Yevgeniy Zateychuk; 203 © Fotolia.com/tairygreene; 204 © Fotolia.com/ivan kmit; 205 © Fotolia.com/Jovan Nikolic; 206 © Fotolia.com/charles taylor; 207 © Fotolia.com/diego cervo; 208 © Fotolia.com/Andrejs Pidjass; 209 © Fotolia.com/aroas; 210 © Fotolia.com/Vibe Images; 211 © Fotolia.com/George Nazmi Bebawi; 212 © Fotolia.com/Phase4Photography; 213 © Fotolia.com/Karin Hildebrand; 214 © Fotolia.com/Anja Kaiser; 215 © Fotolia.com/antipathique; 216 © Fotolia.com/realrock; 217 © Fotolia.com/Dmitriy Rashchektaev; 218 © Fotolia.com/russell witherington; 219 © Fotolia.com/Tan Kian Khoon; 220 © Fotolia.com/Alexander Vasilyev; 221 © Fotolia.com/iofoto; 222 © Fotolia.com/Eric Isselée; 223 © Fotolia.com/Nabok Volodymyr; 224 © Fotolia.com/cwinegarden; 225 © Fotolia.com/Sergey Ilin; 226 © Fotolia.com/petrafler; 227 © Fotolia.com/ultramarin; 228 © Fotolia.com/Oksana Gizima; 229 © Fotolia.com/AndreasG; 230 © Fotolia.com/cienpiesnf; 231 © Fotolia.com/kalafoto; 232 © Fotolia.com/sumos; 233 © Fotolia.com/Sean Gladwell; 234 © Fotolia.com/arquiplay77; 235 © Fotolia.com/Sonar; 236 © Fotolia.com/VIPDesign; 237 © Fotolia.com/DouDou; 238 © Fotolia.com/Ovidiu Iordachi ; 239 © Fotolia.com/Barbara Helgason; 240 © Fotolia.com/AJ; 241 © Fotolia.com/Sharpshot; 242 © Fotolia.com/Adrian Hillman; 243 © Fotolia.com/Stas Perov; 244 © Fotolia.com/charles taylor; 245 © Fotolia.com/Abdelhamid ESSADEL; 246 © Fotolia.com/Nicemonkey; 247 © Fotolia.com/burak duman; 248 © Fotolia.com/Svetlana Romanova; 249 © Fotolia.com/charles taylor; 250 © Fotolia.com/Andrea Danti; 251 © Fotolia.com/Eko Panova; 252 © Fotolia.com/Frank Rohde; 253 © Fotolia.com/Yuri Arcurs; 254 © Fotolia.com/Mitar; 255 © Fotolia.com/sumnersgraphicsinc; 256 © Fotolia.com/Sophie; 257 © Fotolia.com/Dana Heinemann; 258 © iStockphoto.com/Moppet; 259 © Fotolia.com/Photosani; 260 © Fotolia.com/tinadefortunata; 261 © Fotolia.com/Ali Ender Birer; 262 © Fotolia.com/dip; 263 © Fotolia.com/Kwest; 264 © Fotolia.com/NLshop; 265 © Fotolia.com/Zoe; 266 © Fotolia.com/kusuriuri; 267 © Fotolia.com/beaba; 268 © Fotolia.com/Tisskananat; 269 © Fotolia.com/Roman Sigaev; 270 © Fotolia.com/Altay Kaya; 271 © Fotolia.com/christophe BOISSON; 272 © TerriWoesner; 273 © Fotolia.com/Zhanna Ocheret; 274 © Fotolia.com/HerArtSheLoves; 275 © Fotolia.com/Aaron Kohr; 276 © Fotolia.com/gollli; 277 © Fotolia.com/kentoh; 278 © Fotolia.com/notkoo2008; 279 © Fotolia.com/notkoo2008; 280 © Fotolia.com/XtravaganT; 281 © Fotolia.com/Michael Flippo; 282 © Fotolia.com/OnFocus; 283 © Fotolia.com/Andrejs Pidjass; 284 © Fotolia.com/jamesleel; 285 © Fotolia.com/microimages; 286 © Fotolia.com/rosendo; 287 © Fotolia.com/Maksim Samasiuk; 288 © Fotolia.com/mysontuna; 289 © Fotolia.com/Konstantin Sutyagin; 290 © Fotolia.com/fergregory; 291 © Fotolia.com/Michal Adamczyk; 292 © Fotolia.com/Silverpics; 293 © Fotolia.com/Sascha Burkard; 294 © Fotolia.com/L.Bouvier; 295 © Fotolia.com/Stéphane Bidouze; 296 © Fotolia.com/anna_paff; 297 © Fotolia.com/rook76; 298 © Fotolia.com/Michael Brown; 299 © iStockphotos.com/Soubrette; 300 © TerriWoesner; 301 © Fotolia.com/Yuri Arcurs; 302 © Fotolia.com/Pavel Bortel; 303 © Fotolia.com/Sharon Day; 304 © iStockphotos.com/DebbiSmirnoff; 305 © Fotolia.com/festiven; 306 © Fotolia.com/Anja Kaiser; 307 © Fotolia.com/rgbspace; 308 © Fotolia.com/Alexey Potapov; 309 © Fotolia.com/Sunnydays; 310 © Fotolia.com/Cobalt; 311 © Fotolia.com/IKO; 312 © iStockphoto.com/A-Digit; 313 © Fotolia.com/Cheryl Casey; 314 © Fotolia.com/Lvnel; 315 © Fotolia.com/Lvnel; 316 © Fotolia.com/ Bondyman; 317 © Fotolia.com/Carlos Caetano; 318 © TerriWoesner; 319 © Fotolia.com/ Willee Cole; 320 © Fotolia.com/Leyla Medina; 321 © Fotolia.com/Lars Christensen; 322 © Fotolia.com/Ericos; 323 © Fotolia.com/rgbspace; 324 © Fotolia.com/OnFocus; 325 © Fotolia.com/BrandeletDidier; 326 © Fotolia.com/Opla; 327 © iStockphoto.com/Lloret; 328 © Terri Woesner; 329 © Terri Woesner; 330 © Terri Woesner; 331 © Fotolia.com/jcpjr; 332 © iStockphoto.com/MaryLB; 333 © Fotolia.com/Mark Markau; 334 © Terri Woesner; 335 © Terri Woesner; 336 © Fotolia.com/mirpic; 337 © Fotolia.com/LeonART; 338 © Terri Woesner; 339 © Terri Woesner; 340 © Fotolia.com/Stevo; 341 © Fotolia.com/itestro; 342 © iStockphoto.com/filo; 343 © Fotolia.com/Wallyla

Introduction

I was involved in the opening of two restaurants in two years, and we were all new to each other.

I'd wanted a fresh start, so I had a strong feeling of appreciation going into the first job. Around this time, I came across a passage in some reading I had been doing that talked about the principle of giving to those who cannot give back. It struck me that we have all been on the receiving end of some kind of benefit that we could not directly repay, which puts us all in a position of indebtedness. One day, I put this idea to the staff in the form of a question—which would become the first question in this book. Everyone had something to say. Following that day, with rare exception, someone would always ask for the *Question of the Day*.

We all wanted to get to know each other, and *Question of the Day* provided a way for us to be intimate in an intermediate fashion. Over time, relationships grew, times were had, plans were made. Some of us slept together. Some of us wanted to.

Playwright John Patrick Shanley has called theatre "a safe place to do the unsafe things that need to be done." In the same way, you will find that these questions offer you an opportunity to show something about yourself that you don't normally show, a chance to consider your best possible future out loud, and a way to explore something you would like to do, or some new way that you would rather be. *Question of the Day* provides you with a forum to share as much as you would like, and playfully dares you and supports you in going further than you may have intended.

Guidelines

Question of the Day isn't a competitive game with a quantifiable outcome. However, we can all attest that the cliché was never more true than it is here: the more you put into it, the more you will get out of it.

These are the guidelines—not rules, mind you—of *Question of the Day*. There are only a few, and they ensure that you will get the most out of playing.

1. *Question of the Day* is for two or more people to play. When more than two are playing, questions can be asked of the whole group, certain selected people, or just one person.

2. Where more than one person is playing, no one can answer out loud until everyone has thought of his or her best answer. If someone blurts out an answer, it tends to influence everyone else's thinking. The others may try to follow a funny answer with a funny answer of their own, for example, rather than the best answer, or the one that provides the most insight.

3. If someone doesn't have an answer, that's one thing. If someone won't answer, that's quite another. The fact that a person will not answer can be revealing all by itself, and the initial moment when this is stated can be fun. However, the withholding of a juicy answer is unfair to the players who have been forthcoming. The person who won't answer must pay for this by answering the next question, which will be specifically selected for him or her. (On the very rare occasion in which this person will not answer for a second time in a row, I say boot 'em. Any series of nonanswers can easily ruin the vibe of the game. But that's your call.)

4. Whoever is asking the question does not have to answer it. This person is facilitating and can choose to answer, but is not obligated.

5. Many questions allude to persons of influence. Try not to give the answer "my parents" too often, for example. While there are instances in which this can be the best answer, you may provide additional insight into your person by naming someone who influenced you similarly.

6. Some questions have general hints and examples on the same page. These are fair game, to be used at your discretion, but you may want to try to use them only as a last resort. After all, intuition and creativity are a big part of *Question of the Day*. If you do decide to use a hint, repeat the question when you finish reading it.

7. Give people the time they need to answer. If they can't answer, they will let you know. The book is called *Question of the Day* because we would only take on one question a day, sometimes two. Another reason to extend patience is that we have found that people spend a period of time preparing to state the answer out loud after discovering what it is, given that it is sometimes a significant and revealing issue to talk about. The best support you can give is to stand by and let the person work it through.

8. Are people not answering, or giving short answers? Pick lighter questions and have fun with them. This will work people back into the game.

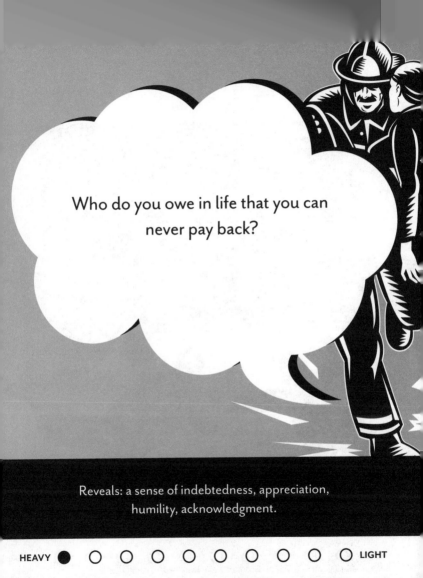

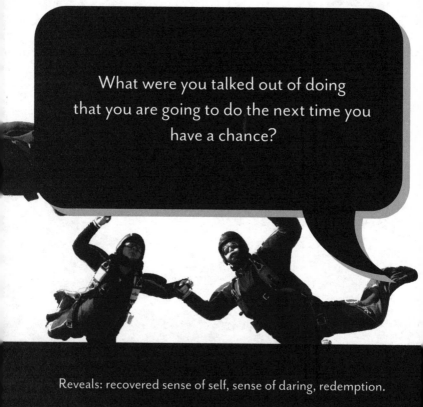

What were you talked out of doing that you are going to do the next time you have a chance?

Reveals: recovered sense of self, sense of daring, redemption.

HEAVY ○ ○ ● ○ ○ ○ ○ ○ ○ ○ LIGHT

What's underrated about you?

What is little known about you that should be better known or get more attention? What don't you get enough credit for?

HEAVY ○ ○ ● ○ ○ ○ ○ ○ ○ ○ LIGHT

What have you done that you previously didn't think you could do?

Remembering having broken new personal ground in the past enables more effective visualization.

HEAVY ○ ○ ○ ● ○ ○ ○ ○ ○ ○ LIGHT

What did you once want a great deal that you do not care about any more?

Reveals: perspective on things we think we want right now.

HEAVY   LIGHT

What person in your life has inspired you to the point of change?

By something that was said to you, by observing a person deal with issues, by being impressed by how far someone has come, or by how they come off.

HEAVY ○ ● ○ ○ ○ ○ ○ ○ ○ ○ LIGHT

What are you tired of
taking the rap for?

Whether true or false. If it's false, everyone should wake up.
If it's true, everyone should get over it.

HEAVY ⚪ ⚪ ⚪ ⚫ ⚪ ⚪ ⚪ ⚪ ⚪ ⚪ LIGHT

Do you make promises?

If "Word Is Bond," why offer insurance? Discuss.

HEAVY ○ ○ ○ ● ○ ○ ○ ○ ○ ○ LIGHT

Where did you once draw the line
that you don't anymore?

Reveals: an opening up of boundaries.

HEAVY   LIGHT

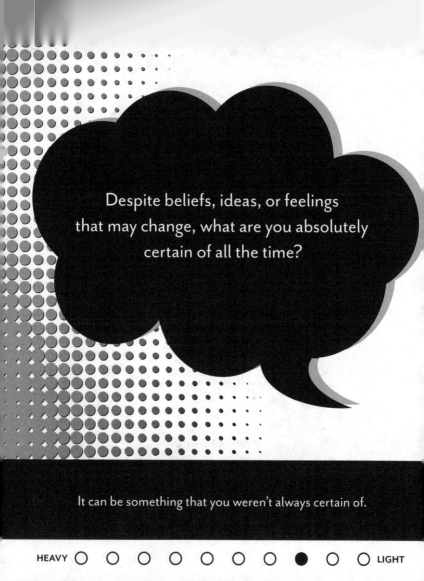

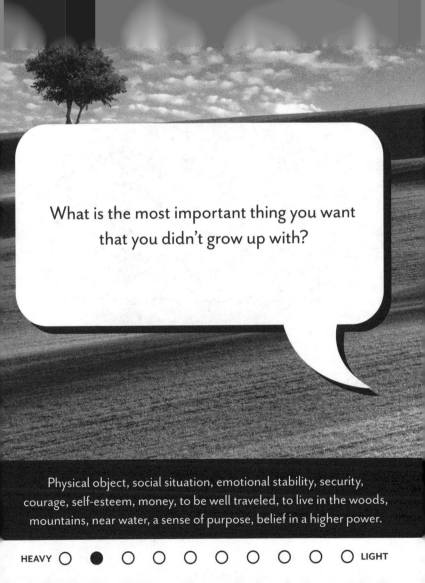

What is the most important thing you want that you didn't grow up with?

Physical object, social situation, emotional stability, security, courage, self-esteem, money, to be well traveled, to live in the woods, mountains, near water, a sense of purpose, belief in a higher power.

HEAVY ○ ● ○ ○ ○ ○ ○ ○ ○ ○ LIGHT

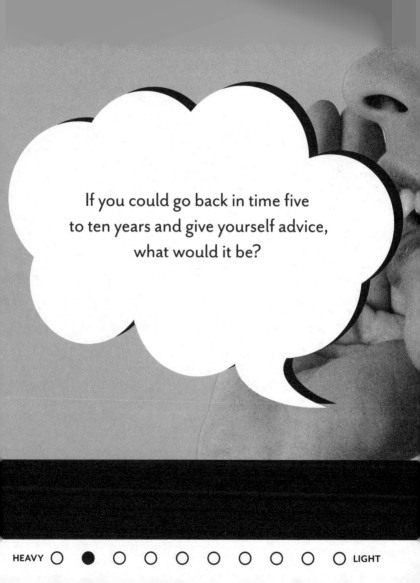

If you could go back in time five to ten years and give yourself advice, what would it be?

HEAVY ○ ● ○ ○ ○ ○ ○ ○ ○ ○ ○ LIGHT

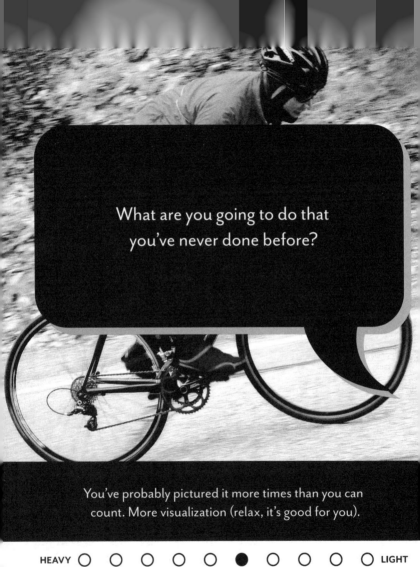

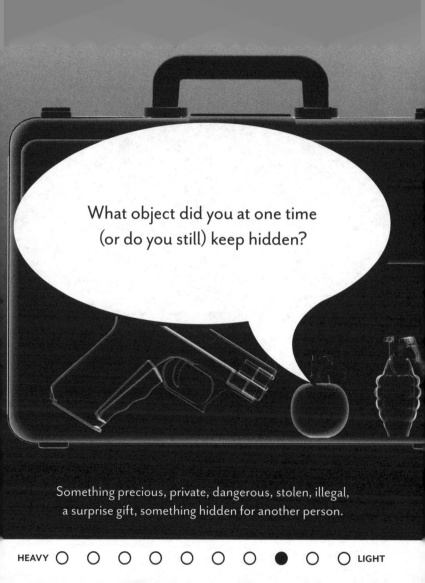

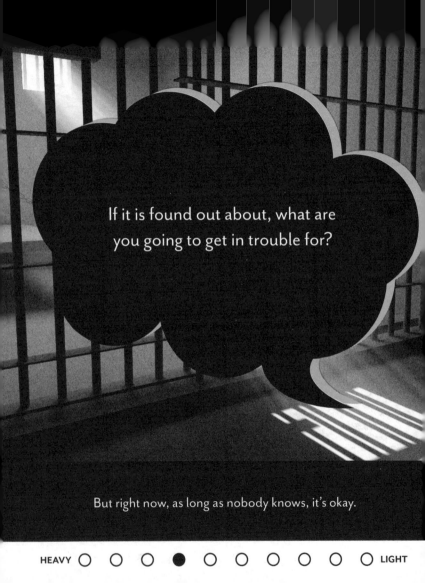

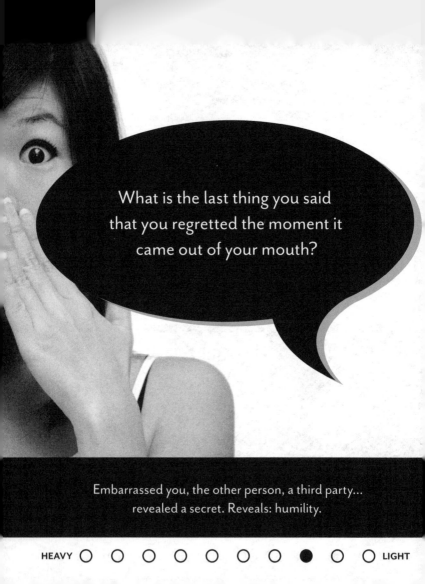

What did you finally do that you should have done a lot sooner than you actually did it?

You kinda knew for a while. This may help you acknowledge your intuition in the future.

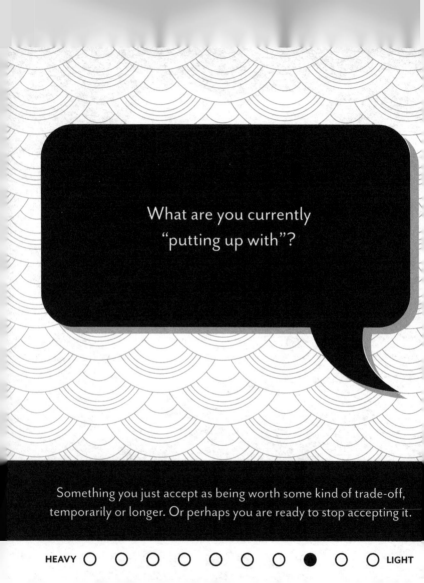

What are you currently "putting up with"?

Something you just accept as being worth some kind of trade-off, temporarily or longer. Or perhaps you are ready to stop accepting it.

HEAVY ○ ○ ○ ○ ○ ○ ○ ● ○ ○ LIGHT

What are you waiting for
the right moment to do?

Be sure you're not just putting it off.

HEAVY ○ ○ ○ ○ ○ ● ○ ○ ○ ○ LIGHT

When did you look back and realize that a long time had felt like a short time to you?

Years seeming like months, months seeming like weeks, hours seeming like minutes. The proverbial "time flies" aspect of perception.

HEAVY ⦿ ⦿ ⦿ ⦿ ⦿ ⦿ ⦿ ⦿ ● ⦿ LIGHT

Who came through for you at a time when you really, really needed it?

Think outside of normal choices. Is there someone you didn't know you could count on until they showed up?

What did you have to give yourself permission to do?

And why? Were you breaking a rule of yours, of someone else's? Were you putting someone out even though it was justified?

HEAVY ○ ○ ○ ● ○ ○ ○ ○ ○ ○ LIGHT

What have you done that you surprised yourself by doing?

Positive or negative. Did you speak up, be more tolerant, snap at someone, do something daring? Reveals: fuller, truer understanding of self.

HEAVY ○ ○ ○ ● ○ ○ ○ ○ ○ ○ LIGHT

What is something you have done that you knew to be right, that another person watching you would see as wrong?

Reveals a sense of conviction, regardless of someone else's ideas or perception.

HEAVY ○ ● ○ ○ ○ ○ ○ ○ ○ ○ LIGHT

What do you owe yourself?

Time, credit, a physical thing, an activity, a break, some fun, relaxation, better conditions, better choices, honesty, another chance, the same slack that you would give someone else.

HEAVY   LIGHT

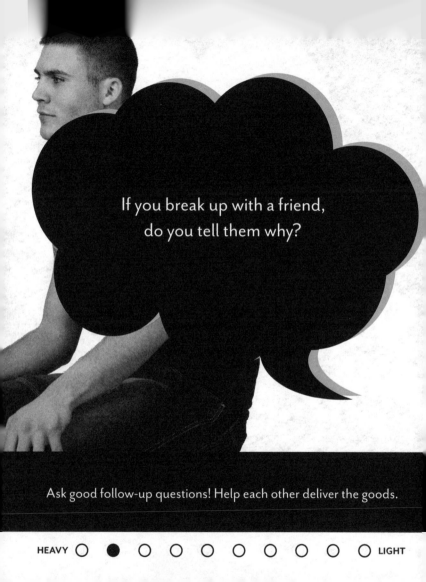

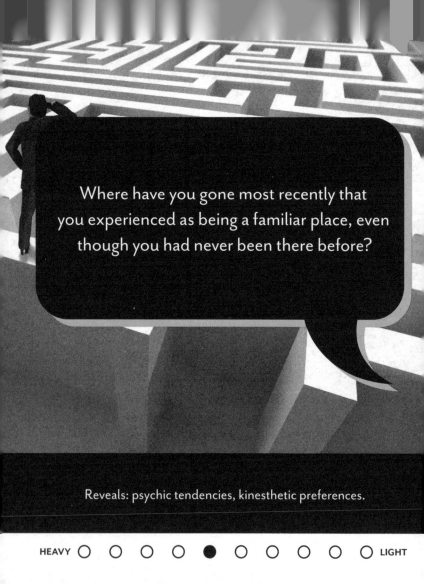

Where do you want to go, even though no one you know is interested in going there with you?

Cool, looks like you're going solo. So, where to?

What do you wish someone
would make you do?

Tell the truth? Face the facts? Something task related?
Something ... adventurous?

HEAVY ○ ○ ○ ● ○ ○ ○ ○ ○ ○ **LIGH**

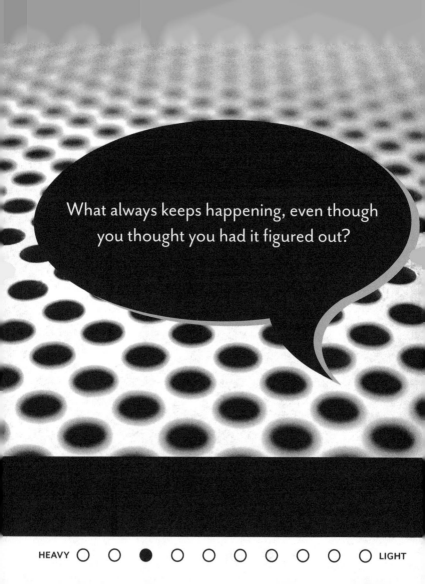

Who are you going to
turn it around with?

This person is far too important to be without,
or to let things stay the way they are now.

HEAVY   LIGHT

What did you get tired of waiting for that you finally went and got somewhere else?

Some aspect of a relationship; job satisfaction; full standing within a group; recognition; energy in the same ratio as you give out.

HEAVY   LIGHT

What do your new friends know about you as a person, see in you, or recognize in you that your old friends have no idea about?

New friends meet the person you've become. In what way have you grown that a long-time friend won't immediately see, acknowledge, or give credit for?

Who owes you, or owed you, an apology, and went about making it up to you in all different ways, but didn't ever actually apologize?

Was it enough? Does that person think it's over and done with? Is it? Was it weird? Was it funny? Did you get angry? Did it work out? Was it lame?

HEAVY ○ ○ ○ ○ ● ○ ○ ○ ○ ○ ○ LIGHT

What have your friends been unable
to convince you to do?

Who is this for? Is this something that's good for you,
or is it something to make them feel better?

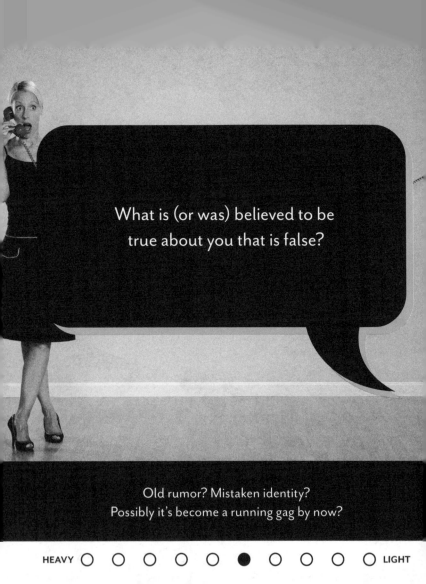

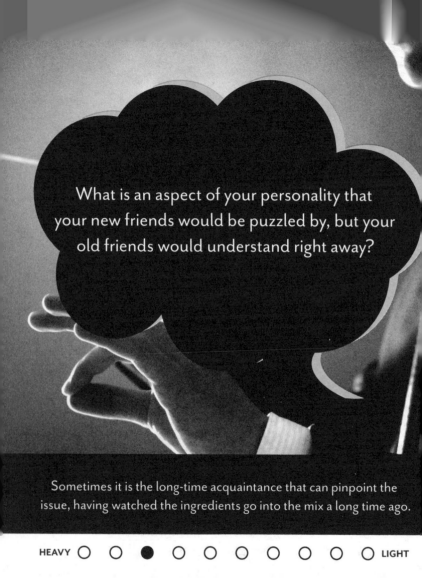

What is an aspect of your personality that your new friends would be puzzled by, but your old friends would understand right away?

Sometimes it is the long-time acquaintance that can pinpoint the issue, having watched the ingredients go into the mix a long time ago.

HEAVY ○ ○ ● ○ ○ ○ ○ ○ ○ ○ LIGHT

What is the last thing you did where you checked to see if anyone was looking ... either before, during, or after?

HEAVY ○ ○ ○ ○ ○ ○ ○ ○ ● ○ LIGHT

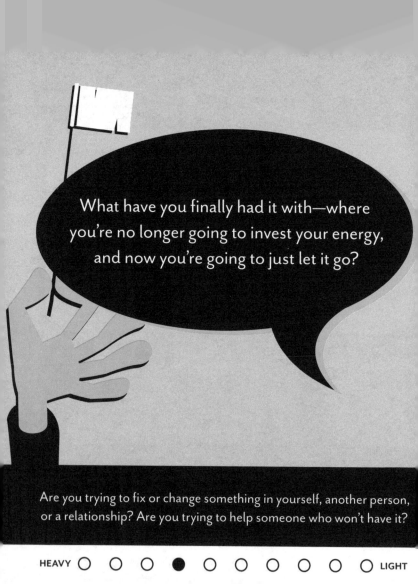

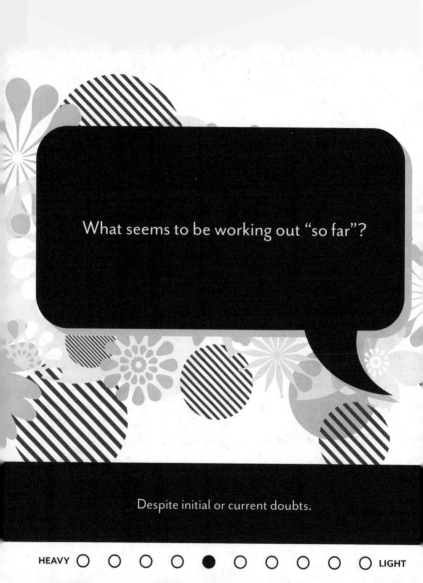

Who are you waiting to hear from?

Maybe you could initiate, but it really is on
the other person at the moment.

HEAVY ○ ○ ○ ○ ○ ○ ● ○ ○ ○ LIGHT

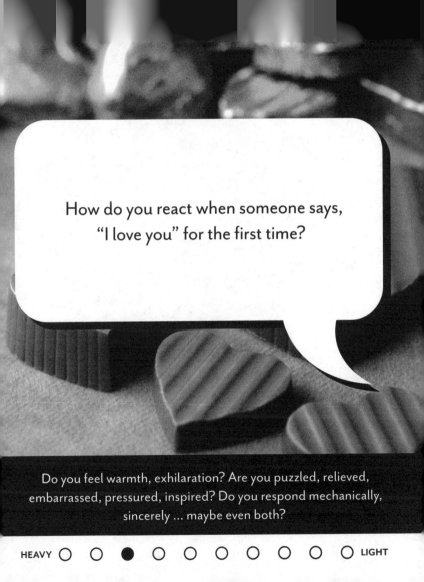

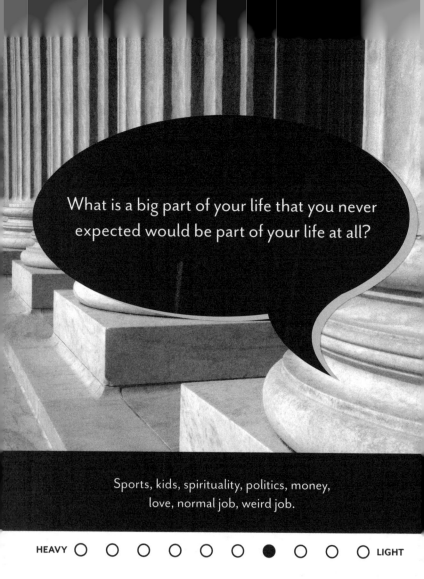

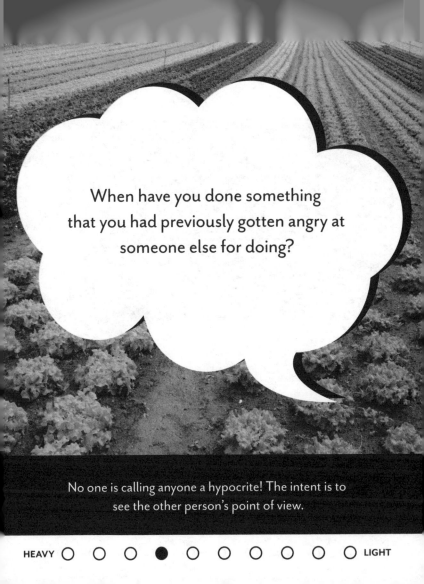

What are you tired of people telling you?

Stop, change, do, care, tell, listen.

HEAVY ○ ○ ○ ○ ○ ○ ● ○ ○ ○ LIGHT

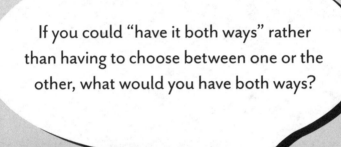

If you could "have it both ways" rather than having to choose between one or the other, what would you have both ways?

Reject the fear of feeling:
a) Greedy; b) Slutty; c) Honest; d) Exposed

HEAVY   LIGHT

Who can't you figure out?

Saying a few things out loud may start to unravel the mystery.

HEAVY ○ ○ ○ ○ ○ ○ ● ○ ○ ○ LIGHT

What comes easily to you that others seem to admire and/or envy?

Take stock of your talents! Remember things that may have been forgotten, or keep things in mind that may be taken for granted.

HEAVY ○ ○ ○ ○ ● ○ ○ ○ ○ ○ LIGHT

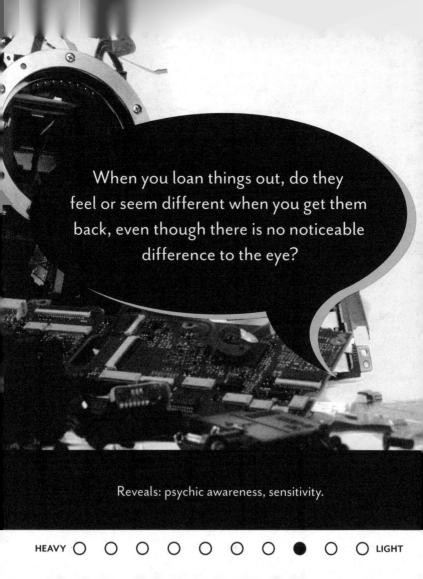

When you loan things out, do they feel or seem different when you get them back, even though there is no noticeable difference to the eye?

Reveals: psychic awareness, sensitivity.

HEAVY ○ ○ ○ ○ ○ ○ ○ ○ ● ○ ○ LIGHT

What is the most socially unacceptable thing that you have no problem with?

Spitting in the street, making out publicly, being loud with one's political opinions.

HEAVY ○ ○ ○ ● ○ ○ ○ ○ ○ ○ LIGHT

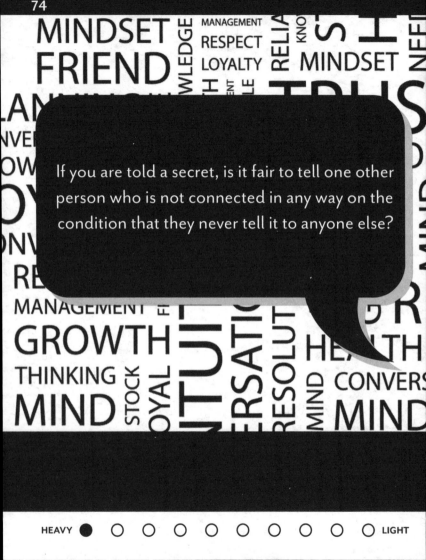

If you are told a secret, is it fair to tell one other person who is not connected in any way on the condition that they never tell it to anyone else?

HEAVY ● ○ ○ ○ ○ ○ ○ ○ ○ ○ ○ LIGHT

Does the news seem like fiction,
or does it seem like part of life?

It is constantly juxtaposed with and presented as entertainment.
Does it all seem like a big story happening somewhere else, to other
people, maybe even at another time? Flesh out your answer.

HEAVY ○ ○ ● ○ ○ ○ ○ ○ ○ ○ LIGHT

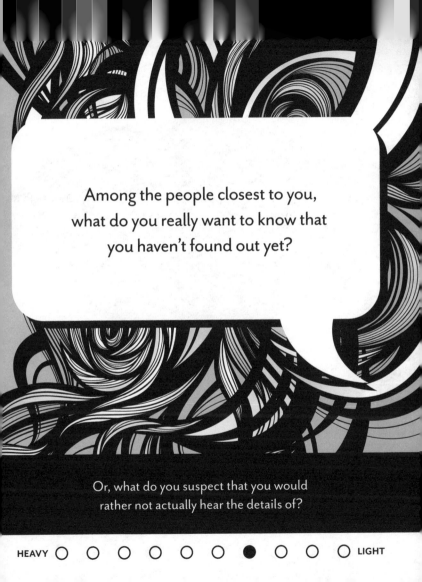

Among the people closest to you, what do you really want to know that you haven't found out yet?

Or, what do you suspect that you would rather not actually hear the details of?

HEAVY ○ ○ ○ ○ ○ ○ ● ○ ○ ○ LIGHT

What habit have you most recently dropped or gotten control over?

Dropped or severely limited. Negated.
Reveals: feeling of control over impulses.

HEAVY ○ ○ ○ ○ ● ○ ○ ○ ○ ○ LIGHT

To what extent do you care
what other people think?

We used to ask, "Do you care what other people think,"
and most people would automatically answer "No"; only to
wind up crumbling under a nominal amount of scrutiny.

HEAVY ○ ○ ● ○ ○ ○ ○ ○ ○ ○ LIGHT

What was the first thing you did
that you said you would never do?

Did you do something wrong, or were your earlier
boundaries too rigid? If you can't name the first thing, just
name something that comes to mind.

HEAVY ○ ○ ○ ● ○ ○ ○ ○ ○ ○ LIGHT

What was your first surreal moment?

One in which you even questioned if it were really going on,
if you were actually dreaming, etc.

HEAVY ◯ ◯ ◯ ◯ ◯ ◯ ● ◯ ◯ ◯ LIGHT

What did you most recently notice someone getting paid for, or doing professionally, that you know you could do better?

You know it, and there's a good reason that you know it.

HEAVY ○ ● ○ ○ ○ ○ ○ ○ ○ ○ LIGHT

What three things will you have to do
to ensure that the next twelve months will be
the best year of your life?

Start that map right now, and then do something toward
one of those three things immediately.

HEAVY ○ ○ ● ○ ○ ○ ○ ○ ○ ○ LIGHT

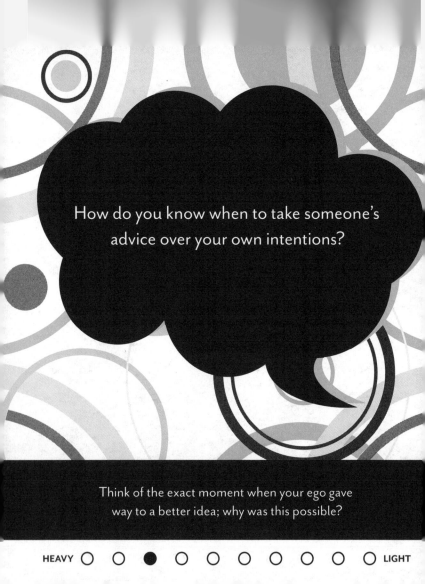

How do you know when to take someone's advice over your own intentions?

Think of the exact moment when your ego gave way to a better idea; why was this possible?

HEAVY ○ ○ ● ○ ○ ○ ○ ○ ○ ○ LIGHT

What's the longest amount of time you've spent doing one thing continuously?

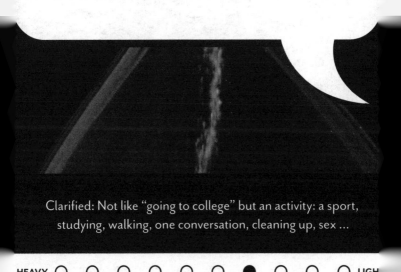

Clarified: Not like "going to college" but an activity: a sport, studying, walking, one conversation, cleaning up, sex …

HEAVY ○ ○ ○ ○ ○ ○ ● ○ ○ ○ LIGH

When have you met someone
for the first time and felt like you've always
known this person?

Take it further. What was the familiar aspect
that made for such an instant affinity?

HEAVY   LIGHT

When did you suddenly feel very much closer to someone you've known for a while, and why?

A traumatic event, important common interests, feelings of empathy, an identical response to an issue.

HEAVY ○ ○ ○ ○ ○ ● ○ ○ ○ ○ LIGHT

What was the last dare you accepted?

And not necessarily in the presence of the dare-er.

When did you last "sneak in" somewhere?

An after-hours swim, an extra helping of movie at the local multiplex, the beach, a schoolyard, your job because you had the keys ...

Who is a kindred spirit to you, and what are the things you have in common?

HEAVY ○ ○ ○ ○ ○ ● ○ ○ ○ LIGHT

What did you recently observe that proves what you've been saying all along?

$$S_\Delta = \sqrt{p(p-a) \cdot (p- \quad -c)} = p$$

$$\frac{2\,tg\,\alpha}{1 - tg^2\alpha}$$

$$\cos\alpha + \cos\beta = 2\cos\frac{\alpha+\beta}{2}\cos\frac{\alpha-\beta}{2}$$

$$\log_a b = \frac{\log}{\log}$$

Have you recently caught yourself saying, "See?!! See that?!!"?
Um, this probably applies to that.

HEAVY ○ ○ ○ ○ ○ ○ ○ ● ○ ○ LIGHT

What traits in your favorite people make you feel that everyone should be that way?

Loyalty, perseverance, a certain temperament, humor, patience, wisdom. Talk about the person; tell a story about the trait.

HEAVY ○ ● ○ ○ ○ ○ ○ ○ ○ ○ ○ LIGHT

What would you be great at that, as of now, you have no intention of doing?

Expand your horizons. Talk about it and enjoy it, see how it feels, enjoy how it feels. Don't be shy about changing some plans.

HEAVY ○ ○ ○ ● ○ ○ ○ ○ ○ ○ LIGHT

What do you firmly believe to be true or right that you feel the world either doesn't know, or doesn't understand?

What do you know that they don't know ... yet.

HEAVY ○ ○ ○ ○ ● ○ ○ ○ ○ ○ ○ LIGHT

What are you done trying to explain to people about yourself?

A trait, something you own, this "one time" when you did something, your music collection, your friends from before ...

HEAVY ○ ○ ○ ● ○ ○ ○ ○ ○ ○ LIGHT

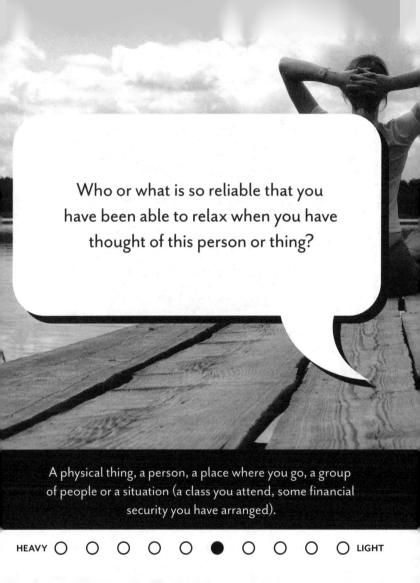

Who or what is so reliable that you have been able to relax when you have thought of this person or thing?

A physical thing, a person, a place where you go, a group of people or a situation (a class you attend, some financial security you have arranged).

HEAVY ○ ○ ○ ○ ○ ● ○ ○ ○ ○ LIGHT

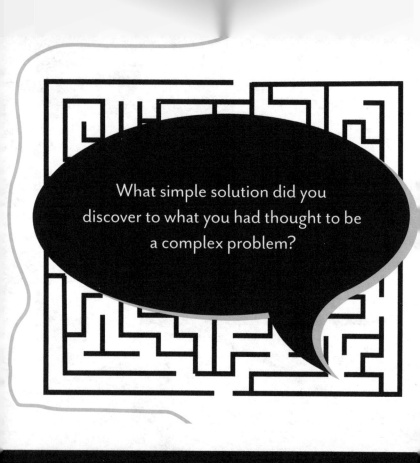

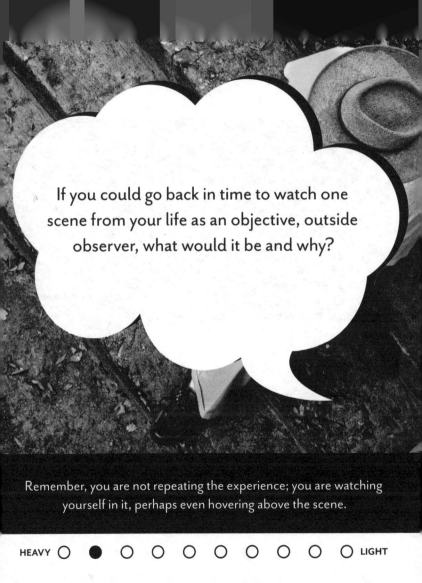

Do you love the present more than the past?

Fess up for now ... and work on how you
think it "should" be afterwards.

HEAVY ○ ○ ○ ● ○ ○ ○ ○ ○ ○ LIGHT

Will you lie for a friend?

HEAVY ○ ○ ○ ○ ● ○ ○ ○ ○ ○ LIGHT

At what point is loyalty too much to ask?

A test of boundaries and rules. Follow-up questions are important here. Get great answers from each other.

HEAVY ○ ○ ● ○ ○ ○ ○ ○ ○ ○ LIGHT

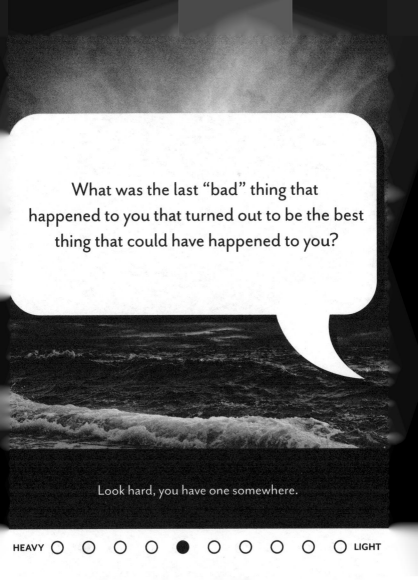

What was the last "bad" thing that happened to you that turned out to be the best thing that could have happened to you?

Look hard, you have one somewhere.

HEAVY ○ ○ ○ ○ ● ○ ○ ○ ○ ○ LIGHT

If you are not only suspected of something, but are genuinely believed to be guilty, and will always be treated as guilty, should you go ahead and do it anyway?

You may have considered it already ...

HEAVY ○ ○ ○ ○ ○ ○ ○ ○ ● ○ LIGHT

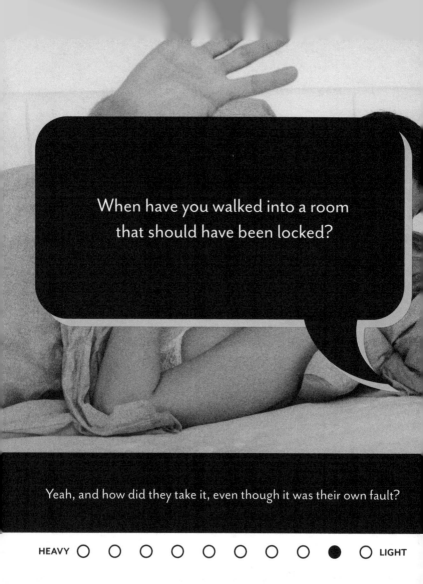

What's the best physical object that you kept or "wound up with" from a previous relationship?

Not a gift to you, a former personal possession of the other person.

HEAVY ○ ○ ○ ○ ○ ○ ○ ○ ● ○ LIGHT

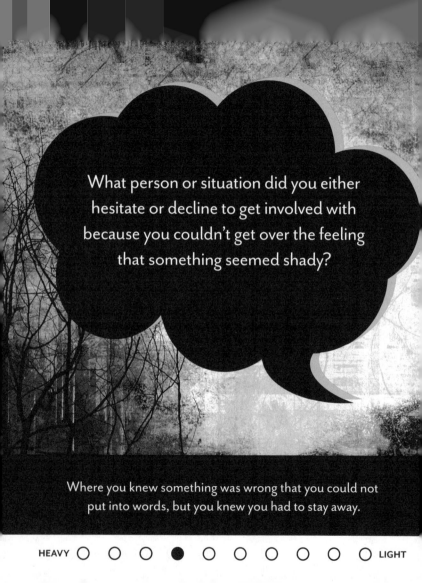

What person or situation did you either hesitate or decline to get involved with because you couldn't get over the feeling that something seemed shady?

Where you knew something was wrong that you could not put into words, but you knew you had to stay away.

HEAVY ○ ○ ○ ● ○ ○ ○ ○ ○ ○ LIGHT

What were you most recently watching on TV by yourself that you changed the channel on when someone else came into the room?

Come on, it's just a big shame box, anyway. Tell us!

HEAVY ○ ○ ○ ○ ○ ○ ○ ○ ○ ● LIGHT

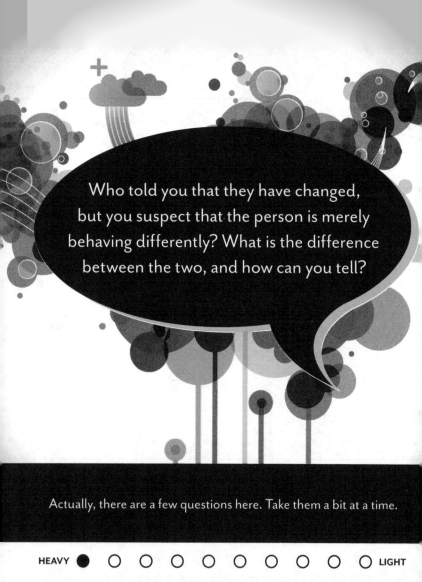

Who told you that they have changed, but you suspect that the person is merely behaving differently? What is the difference between the two, and how can you tell?

Actually, there are a few questions here. Take them a bit at a time.

HEAVY ●〇〇〇〇〇〇〇〇〇 〇 LIGHT

What's the first movie you saw that you were too young to see?

Right, and were you with family? That's a whole other level.

HEAVY ○ ○ ○ ○ ○ ○ ○ ○ ○ ● LIGHT

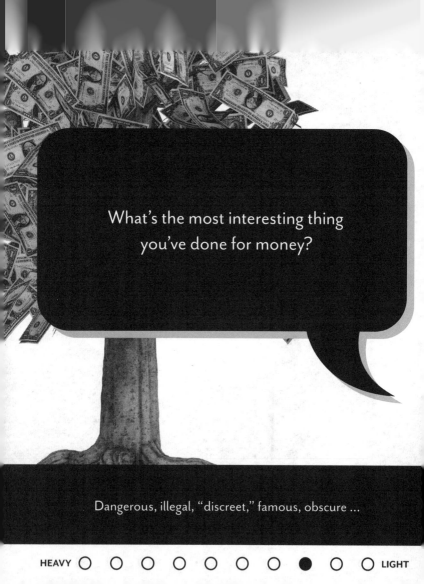

Who is the last person
you went to with a problem who made
you feel that they would stay with you for as long
as it took: not pull away, not end the
conversation, not excuse themselves, or
not hang up the phone ...
until you were done?

That's someone you can never repay. See Question 1.

HEAVY ○ ● ○ ○ ○ ○ ○ ○ ○ ○ ○ LIGHT

What is missing from your life that you used to get from a person you are no longer around, no longer with, or cannot be with?

By the way, the idea is to reconnect with the positive feeling so you can go do something about it.

HEAVY ○ ● ○ ○ ○ ○ ○ ○ ○ ○ LIGHT

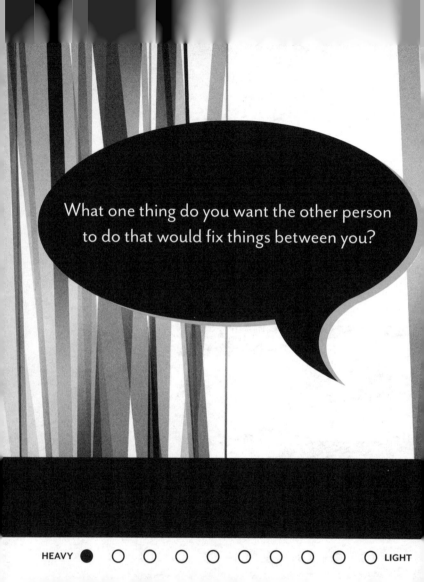

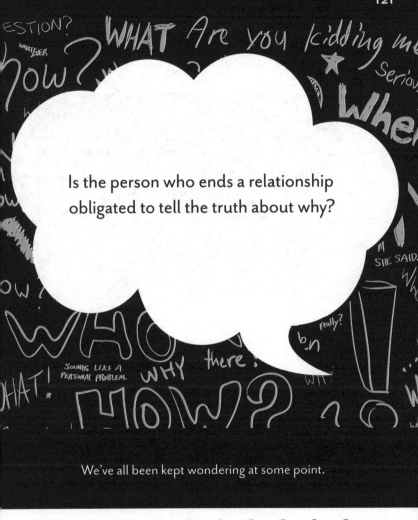

Is the person who ends a relationship obligated to tell the truth about why?

We've all been kept wondering at some point.

HEAVY ○ ● ○ ○ ○ ○ ○ ○ ○ ○ LIGHT

To what extent can you be counted on?

Do you have a general answer, or is it conditional?

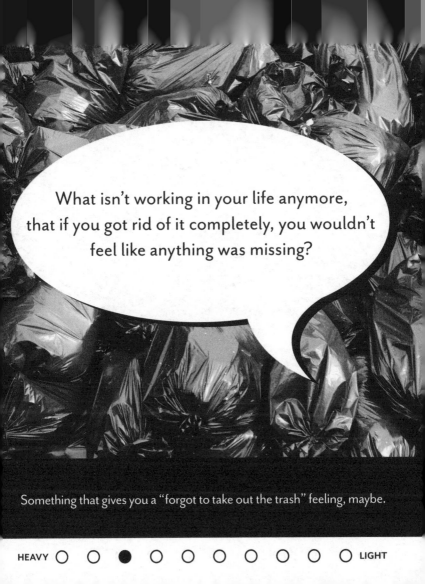

What is a quality that people keep
saying you have, but you aren't ready to own
or accept completely?

Are you shy about it? Does it make you uncomfortable? Are you
better at something than someone you are fond of?

HEAVY   LIGHT

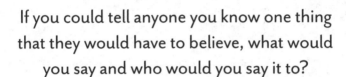

If you could tell anyone you know one thing that they would have to believe, what would you say and who would you say it to?

A fact, thought, or idea that you feel would make a significant difference in another person's life.

HEAVY ○ ○ ● ○ ○ ○ ○ ○ ○ ○ LIGHT

When did you decide wrongly about someone?

Could be over a single incident, could be what you thought of them overall. Why the change in attitude/opinion, by the way?

HEAVY ○ ○ ○ ○ ○ ● ○ ○ ○ ○ LIGHT

Why are your friends friends with you?

What do they get out of your friendship?

What do you now think is possible in your life that would have seemed impossible five years ago?

Even considering it would have been like reading fiction.

HEAVY ○ ● ○ ○ ○ ○ ○ ○ ○ ○ LIGHT

Often, we hear people saying,
"Everything happens for a reason."
What do you think? Does it?

Beyond the basic idea of cause and effect, many people
imply a cosmic connection when saying this.

HEAVY ○ ○ ○ ○ ○ ○ ○ ● ○ ○ LIGHT

What did you secretly hope or believe about yourself that you were more fully able to believe after someone pointed it out?

Outside validation is something we don't like to court, but it can help at the right moment.

HEAVY ○ ○ ○ ● ○ ○ ○ ○ ○ ○ **LIGHT**

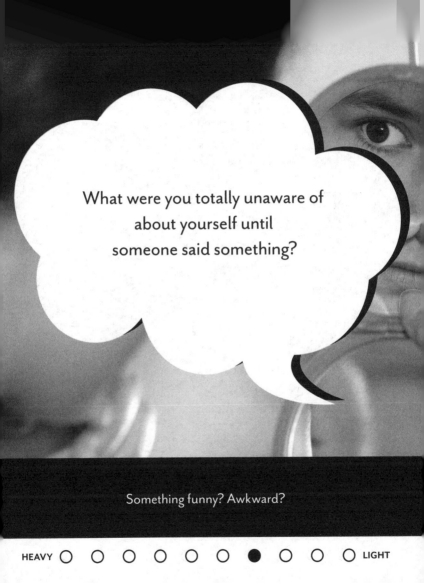

What were you totally unaware of about yourself until someone said something?

Something funny? Awkward?

HEAVY ○ ○ ○ ○ ○ ○ ● ○ ○ ○ LIGHT

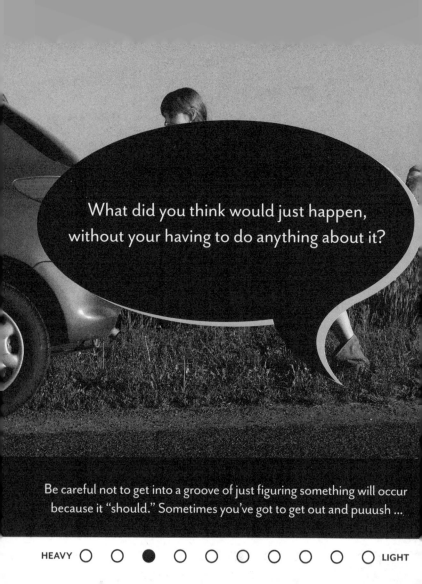

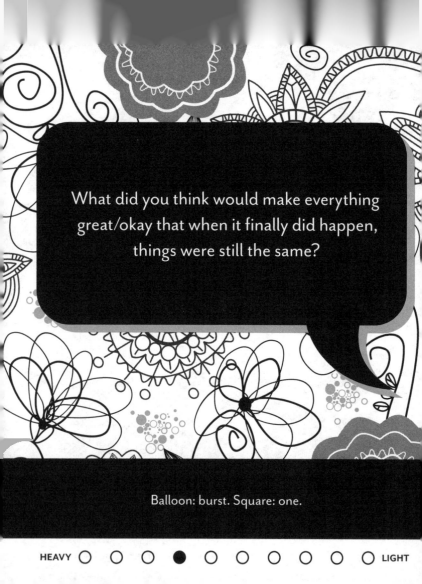

What did you think would make everything great/okay that when it finally did happen, things were still the same?

Balloon: burst. Square: one.

HEAVY ○ ○ ○ ● ○ ○ ○ ○ ○ ○ LIGHT

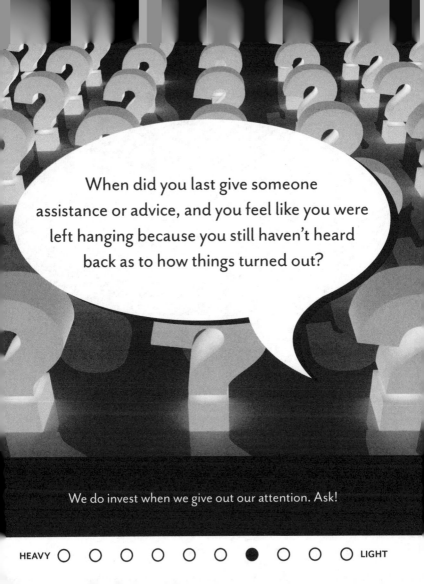

What were you annoyed at being reminded of that you were later glad to have been reminded of?

Irritation is temporary. Going back inside and unplugging the iron is a gift that keeps on giving.

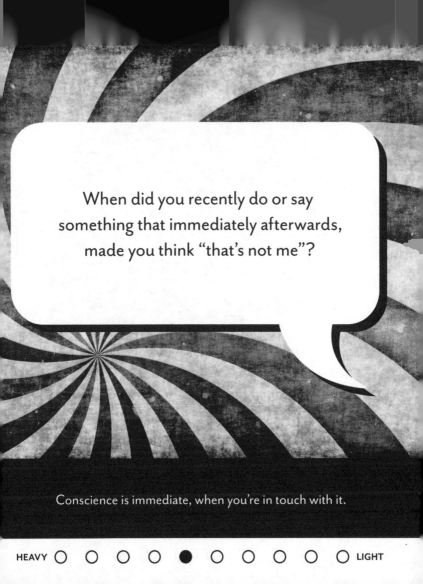

When did you recently do or say something that immediately afterwards, made you think "that's not me"?

Conscience is immediate, when you're in touch with it.

HEAVY ○ ○ ○ ○ ● ○ ○ ○ ○ ○ LIGHT

What is the most recent thing you did to help that you know won't be appreciated, or noticed right away ... but you don't care?

HEAVY ○ ○ ○ ○ ○ ○ ○ ○ ● ○ ○ LIGHT

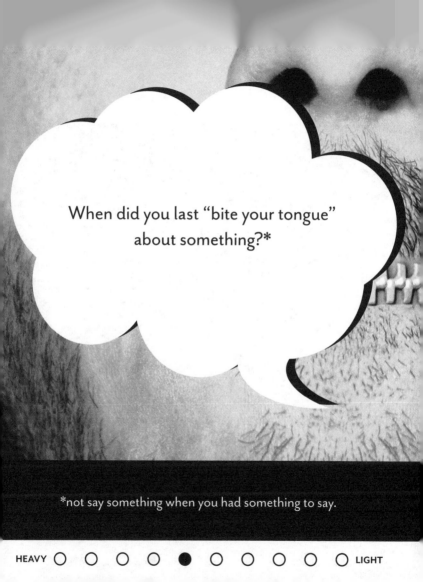

Who has startled you by saying something to you that you always thought to be true, but have never said out loud?

That funny, crazy feeling that someone else is inside your head ...

What does no one seem to agree
with you about?

Commitment can be a lonely path. It sucks to be right, sometimes!

HEAVY ○ ○ ○ ○ ○ ○ ● ○ ○ ○ ○ LIGHT

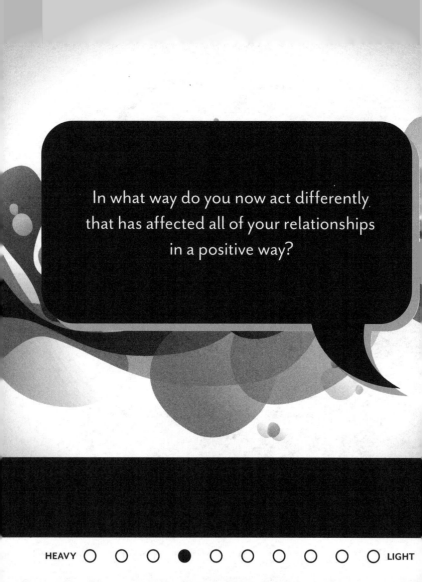

Does relying on someone
make you feel vulnerable?

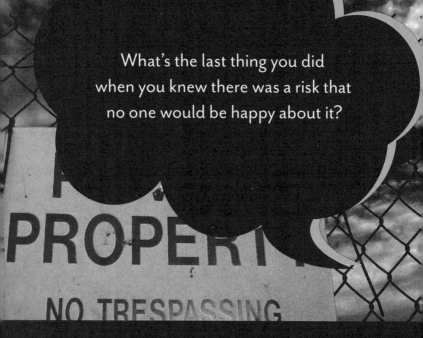

What's the last thing you did
when you knew there was a risk that
no one would be happy about it?

The R word again. You are using it wisely I take it?

HEAVY ○ ○ ○ ● ○ ○ ○ ○ ○ ○ LIGHT

What is the most recent gift you received
that you were dishonest about
how much you liked it?

You are a decent-sized hero, accepting that piece of junk and then
worrying how they feel about it. VIP in the afterlife for you.

HEAVY ◯ ◯ ◯ ◯ ◯ ● ◯ ◯ ◯ ◯ LIGHT

When did you last think someone was being serious, but they said they were only kidding and it became a whole thing?

STRIKE OU

I mean, it does happen, but there are always people who regularly play both sides. They need a three-strike rule. Meanwhile, you have a definite type of situation on your hands.

HEAVY ○ ○ ○ ● ○ ○ ○ ○ ○ ○ LIGHT

What can't you go forward with until the other person does something?

HEAVY ○ ○ ○ ○ ● ○ ○ ○ ○ ○ LIGHT

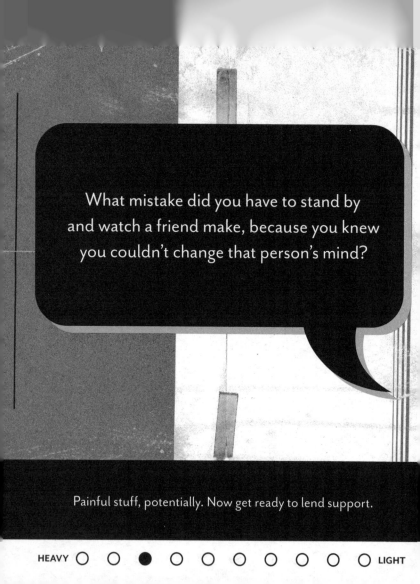

What mistake did you have to stand by and watch a friend make, because you knew you couldn't change that person's mind?

Painful stuff, potentially. Now get ready to lend support.

HEAVY ○ ○ ● ○ ○ ○ ○ ○ ○ ○ LIGHT

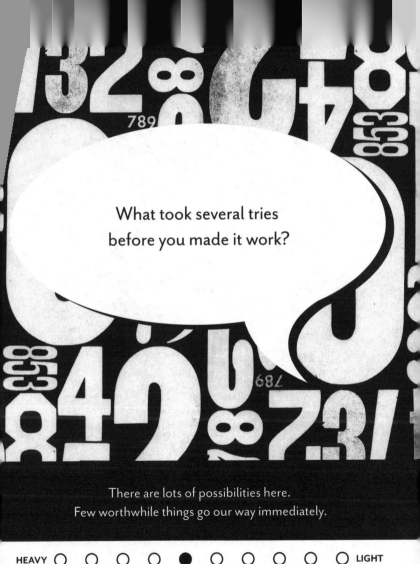

What took several tries
before you made it work?

There are lots of possibilities here.
Few worthwhile things go our way immediately.

HEAVY ○ ○ ○ ○ ● ○ ○ ○ ○ ○ LIGHT

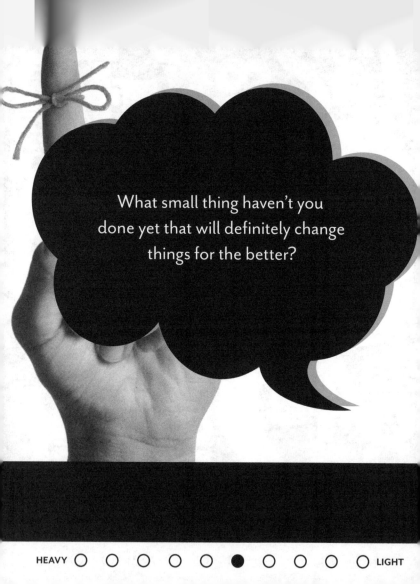

What is a band, artist, or TV show
that you "do alone" (no one else that you
know seems to be interested)?

That can get interesting.
You do wind up meeting new people that way, as well.

HEAVY   LIGHT

What's the best thing that could happen in your life if fear had no effect on you whatsoever?

Take a serious moment to answer this question, and then look at how much you are or may be losing out on. This is a great opportunity to gain some perspective.

HEAVY ● ○ ○ ○ ○ ○ ○ ○ ○ ○ LIGHT

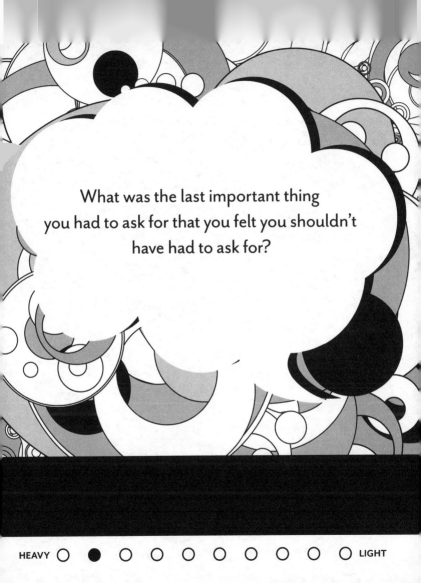

What's a positive aspect of your personality that came into existence because of a relationship with someone else?

Did they loosen you up, give you confidence, reinforce some aspect that was already on the rise?

HEAVY ○ ○ ○ ● ○ ○ ○ ○ ○ ○ LIGHT

When did you most recently listen to a friend that came to you with an issue and find it to be too much, even though you previously told them that they could always come to you with anything?

Good friends always make that big offer. Then, you sometimes need a friend to help you be friends with your friend. Life is like that.

HEAVY   LIGHT

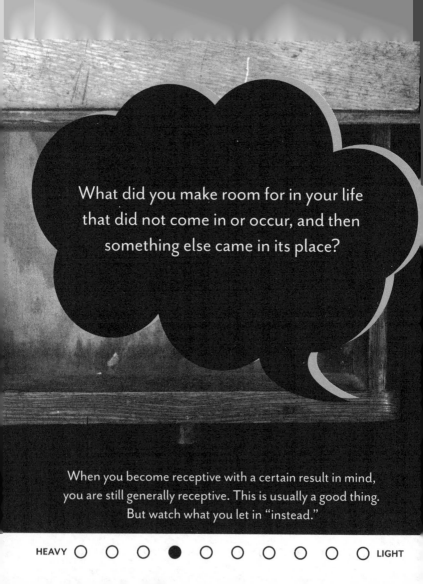

What did you make room for in your life that did not come in or occur, and then something else came in its place?

When you become receptive with a certain result in mind, you are still generally receptive. This is usually a good thing. But watch what you let in "instead."

HEAVY ○ ○ ○ ● ○ ○ ○ ○ ○ ○ LIGHT

Who will always be completely truthful with you, whether you want to hear it or not?

Sometimes you have to avoid that person for a day, right?
Still, it's a good thing that they are around.

HEAVY ○ ○ ○ ○ ● ○ ○ ○ ○ ○ LIGHT

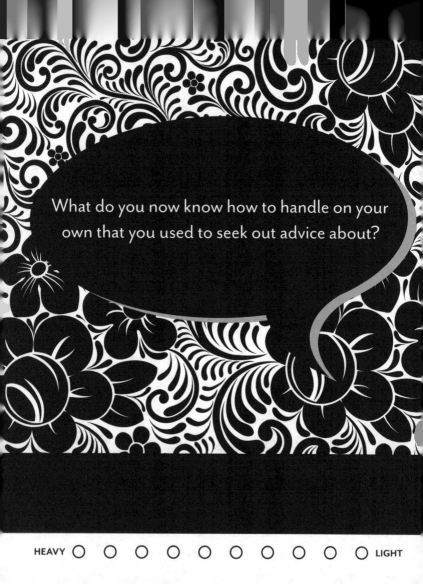

What do you now know how to handle on your own that you used to seek out advice about?

What gift or other offering did you turn down because it was out of proportion?

Sometimes, when two people like each other, one person really likes the other person. A little extra. Awkward, common, etc. Not always fixable, but go forward with love (the right amount).

HEAVY   LIGHT

Without anyone else prompting you, when did you know it was time to stop?

The famous "moment of clarity" applies to so many things. Did you have one?

HEAVY ○ ○ ● ○ ○ ○ ○ ○ ○ ○ LIGHT

A lot of things, or not as many as most people do? Emotional support, conversation? Or is it basically just down to infrastructure and groceries?

HEAVY ○ ● ○ ○ ○ ○ ○ ○ ○ ○ LIGHT

Who told you so, but you never listened, and then you had to find out for yourself?

"Told ya so" sucks, but at least someone tried to tell you up front.

HEAVY ○ ○ ○ ○ ○ ○ ○ ○ ● ○ LIGHT

When did you remove yourself from drama?

Can everyone just learn to focus on issues without coming down with a case of Diva-itis?

HEAVY   LIGHT

What do you suspect that you'd rather not know about?

HEAVY ○ ○ ○ ● ○ ○ ○ ○ ○ ○ LIGHT

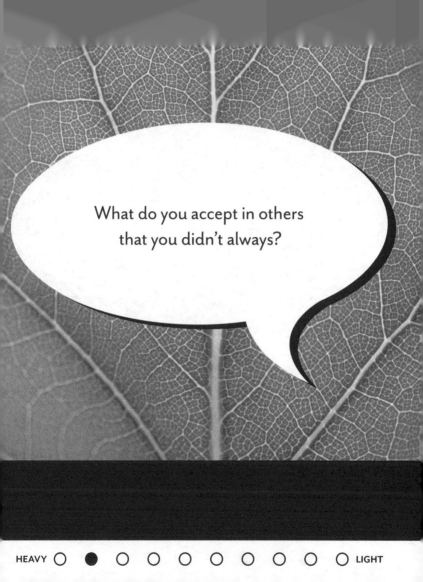

What place or activity always makes you think of a certain person?

They probably think of you, too.

HEAVY ○ ○ ○ ○ ○ ● ○ ○ ○ ○ LIGHT

What finally changed in your favor after you'd (totally) given up hope?

Something you worked on? Someone? Did you ask?
Did you say nothing?

What's the most recent thing you did that afterwards made you say or think, "I hope somebody saw that..."?

Even a waste paper basket shot from three-point land wants a little acknowledgment.

HEAVY ○ ○ ○ ○ ○ ○ ● ○ ○ ○ LIGHT

What is a great place to go that, so far, is not spoiled by too many people knowing about it?

.

Your haven. Let's face it, there's always the next version of the tree house. Take care in exposing your oasis.

HEAVY   LIGHT

Over time, have you grown more towards relying on yourself, or relying more on others?

Independence and interdependence. We need them both. Which way do you lean?

HEAVY ○ ● ○ ○ ○ ○ ○ ○ ○ ○ LIGHT

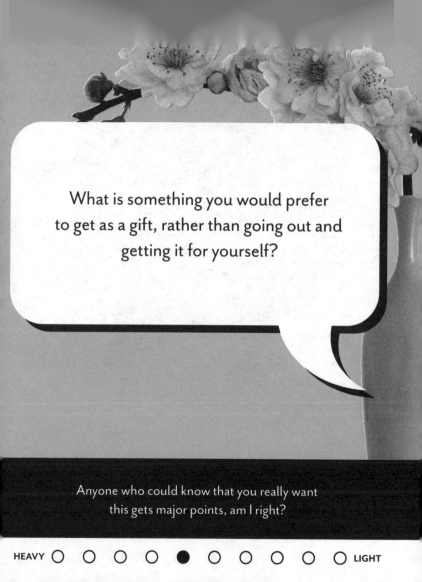

Who did you learn from even though you can't stand them?

HEAVY ○ ○ ● ○ ○ ○ ○ ○ ○ ○ LIGHT

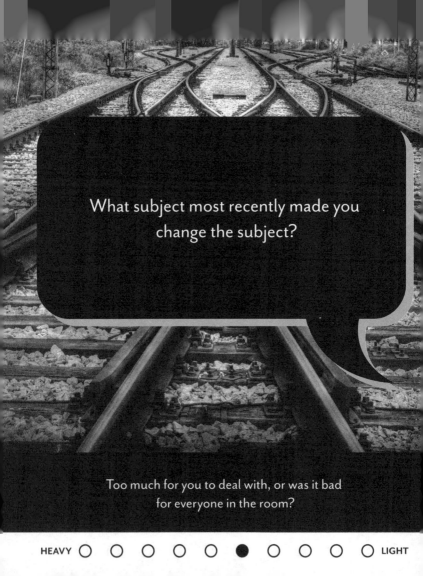

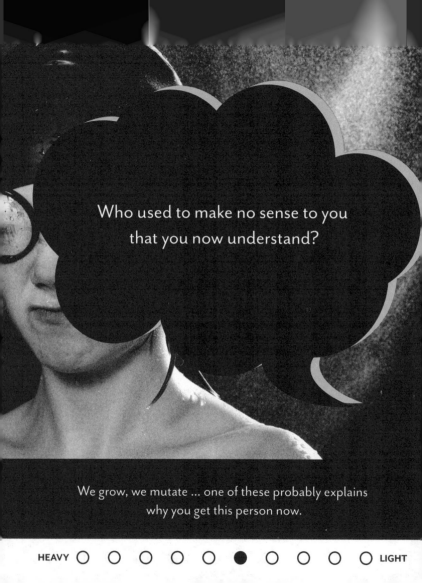

What's the last thing everyone in the room was doing that you were pretty much expected to do also ... and you didn't do it?

Social packs and tribes have no idea how they're acting, sometimes. They demand things to define the group, and to strengthen the leaders. Kudos for resisting. Tell your story proudly.

HEAVY ● ○ ○ ○ ○ ○ ○ ○ ○ ○ LIGHT

What part of technology or modern life takes too much away from people (either by doing too much of their work for them or by limiting their imagination)?

Part of a long tradition of "no one admits it, but everyone knows it's true."

HEAVY   LIGHT

When did you help someone out and expect to feel great about it, but you felt nothing instead?

Confusing, huh? Maybe your motives weren't so pure.
So what? You did a good thing.

What do you wish you had an internal alarm for, so that you could be reminded to do or not do, or say or not say, some particular thing?

Potentially juicy question! And what happened last time this alarm was unavailable?

HEAVY ○ ○ ○ ● ○ ○ ○ ○ ○ ○ LIGHT

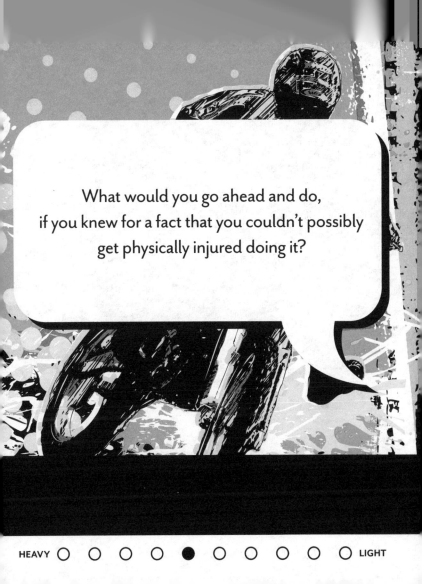

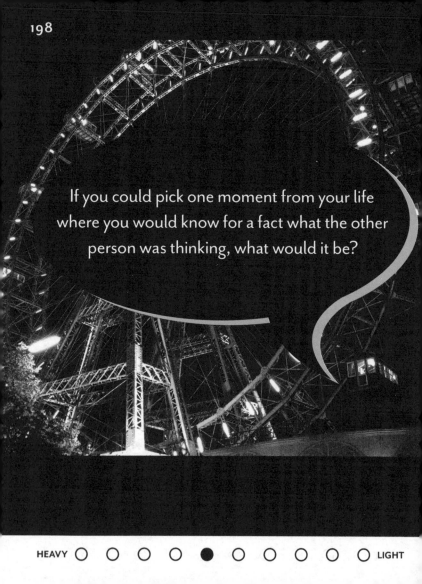

If you could pick one moment from your life where you would know for a fact what the other person was thinking, what would it be?

HEAVY ○ ○ ○ ○ ● ○ ○ ○ ○ ○ LIGHT

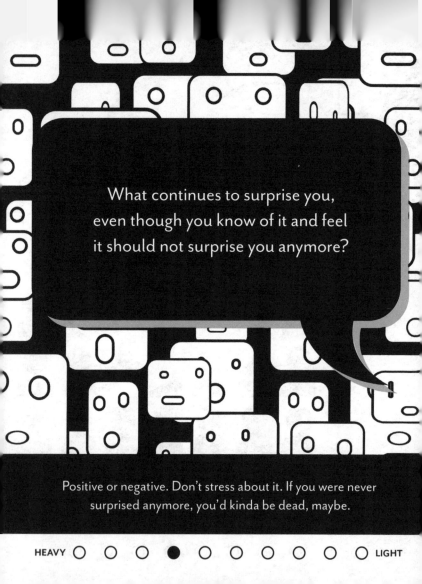

What do you keep doing that if you saw
a friend doing it, you would try to stop them,
or at least say something?

Will it make you think twice before you do it again?
Or is it "okay" when you do it?

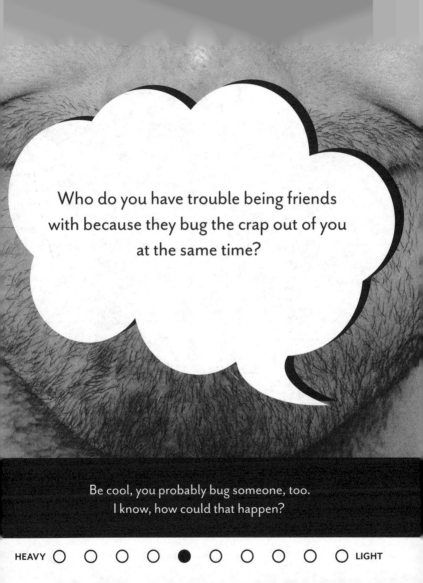

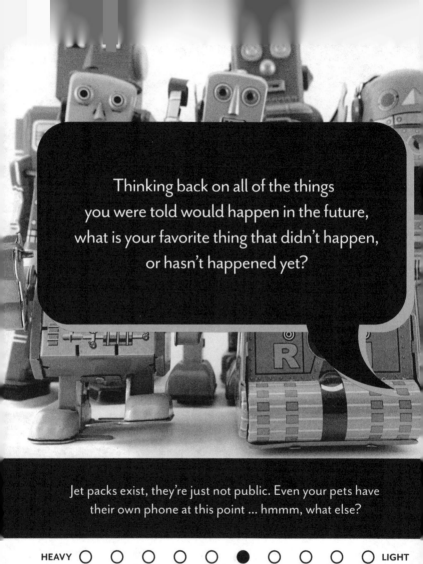

Thinking back on all of the things you were told would happen in the future, what is your favorite thing that didn't happen, or hasn't happened yet?

Jet packs exist, they're just not public. Even your pets have their own phone at this point ... hmmm, what else?

HEAVY ○ ○ ○ ○ ○ ● ○ ○ ○ ○ LIGHT

How long do you wait until you declare somebody to be late, and then how long until you get angry about it?

Granted, you get to be right, but can you avoid making it worse?

HEAVY ○ ○ ○ ○ ○ ○ ○ ● ○ ○ ○ LIGHT

Who have you gone to for advice that, admittedly, can't even get their own shit together?

Do you avoid telling other people who gave you this advice?
There's a clue for you!

HEAVY   LIGHT

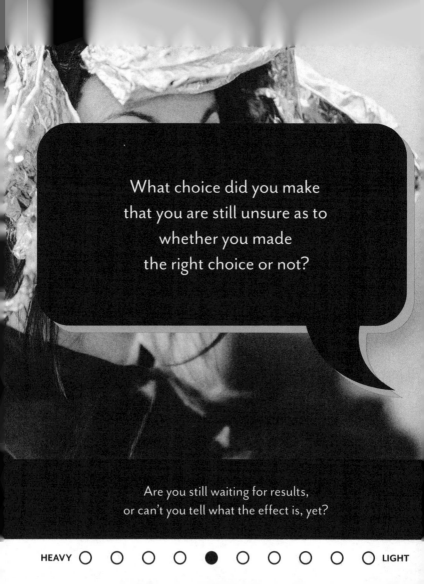

What were you brought up to believe about life that you found to be untrue in your own experience?

Maybe it took a while for you to acknowledge the clash. Was there a floodgate after the first one?

HEAVY   LIGHT

What new store won't you go into
because of what the previous store
in the same location had been?

OPEN

In my old neighborhood, a diner replaced a pet store. NO WAY.

HEAVY ○ ○ ○ ○ ○ ○ ○ ○ ○ ● LIGHT

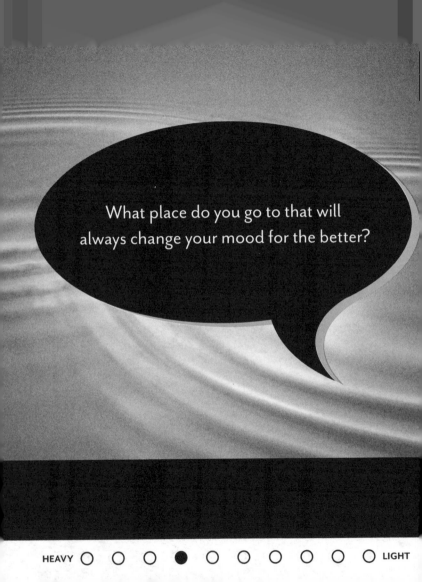

What had you always heard about that shocked you when you finally experienced it for yourself?

The words of others can't really prepare you for the moment, can they?

HEAVY ○ ○ ○ ○ ● ○ ○ ○ ○ ○ LIGHT

Tell a story from your life
that you've never told.

Yeah, okay, okay ... it's not a question. Do it!

HEAVY ○ ● ○ ○ ○ ○ ○ ○ ○ ○ LIGHT

What overall situation or specific incident was never explained to you that had a major impact on how you grew up?

Do you need to understand? Do you need to let it go?

HEAVY   LIGHT

What is the most common trait
amongst your friends?

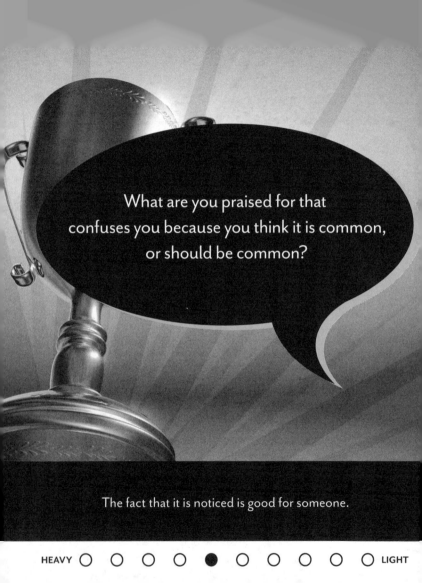

What should you have seen coming?

Review the warning signs; next time you'll have intuition in your utility belt, ready to go.

HEAVY ○ ○ ○ ○ ○ ● ○ ○ ○ ○ LIGHT

Who or what did you not realize you were attached to until that person or thing was gone?

This is a little variation on the old cliché.

HEAVY ○ ○ ○ ○ ○ ● ○ ○ ○ ○ LIGHT

What experience made you realize that you can do more than you had previously thought?

Did someone help by pushing you further than you may have gone? Did you have to make up for someone's absence? Did you get in over your head and make the most of it? Or did you just demand more of yourself?

HEAVY   LIGHT

What issue from your life do your friends quickly/always claim they would have handled differently, even though they have no real grasp of the situation?

"Oh, I would never have done that." Yeah, I know. You're so much better at being me than I am ...

When were you told a secret that you felt was wrong or unfair for you to have to keep?

Something you felt unfairly burdened by.

HEAVY ○ ○ ○ ○ ● ○ ○ ○ ○ ○ LIGHT

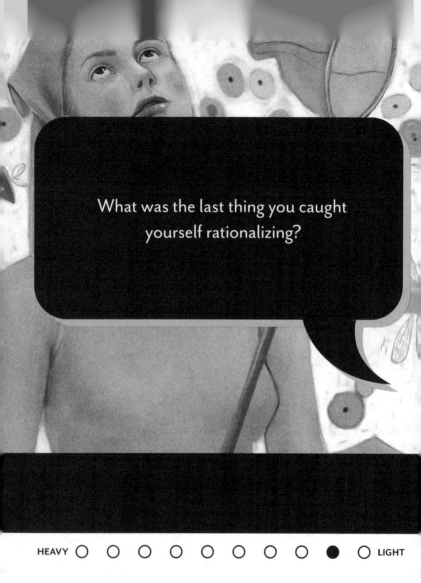

What was the last thing you caught yourself rationalizing?

HEAVY ○ ○ ○ ○ ○ ○ ○ ○ ● ○ LIGHT

What were your friends right about that you haven't admitted to them?

(Yet)

HEAVY ○ ○ ○ ○ ○ ○ ○ ● ○ ○ LIGHT

When was your loyalty to a friend compromised because you also became friends with their significant other?

Something is gained, and something is lost. Does it even out? Describe both.

HEAVY   LIGHT

What event did you get almost nothing out of because you had something else on your mind the whole time?

Sigh ... you probably paid for tickets, too, didn't you? AND couldn't keep up with the discussion about it afterwards. Great ...

HEAVY   ●   LIGHT

Who still feels that you owe them,
even though you've
made it up to them repeatedly?

Some people treat their hurts like bruises that they
won't allow to heal. You'll never be able to do "enough."
Let it go, you've done your part.

HEAVY ○ ○ ○ ○ ● ○ ○ ○ ○ ○ LIGHT

What do you have to be patient about, even though you can't stand being patient about it?

That's because patience suuuucks! It also yields more positive results than almost anything else you can consciously practice. Hang in there.

HEAVY ○ ○ ○ ○ ● ○ ○ ○ ○ ○ LIGHT

Of the people you know, who is "crazy"
in a good way, and who is "crazy" in a bad way?

You know ... "Inspiring and uninhibited" on one side,
and "restraining order" on the other side.

What rules did you grow up with that you later found to be too limiting?

Family rules, teacher rules, pseudoreligious rules, library rules, cafeteria rules ...

HEAVY ○ ○ ○ ○ ● ○ ○ ○ ○ ○ LIGHT

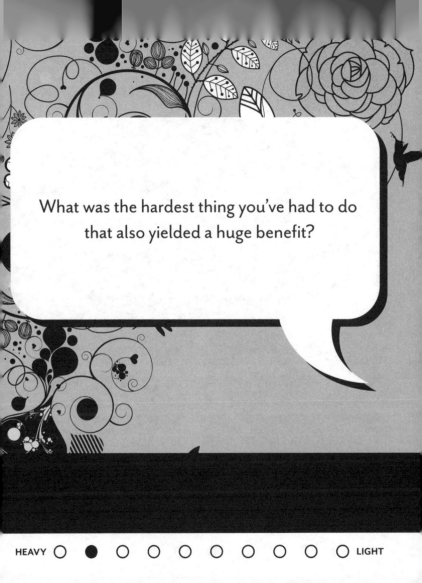

What was the hardest thing you've had to do
that also yielded a huge benefit?

HEAVY ○ ● ○ ○ ○ ○ ○ ○ ○ ○ LIGHT

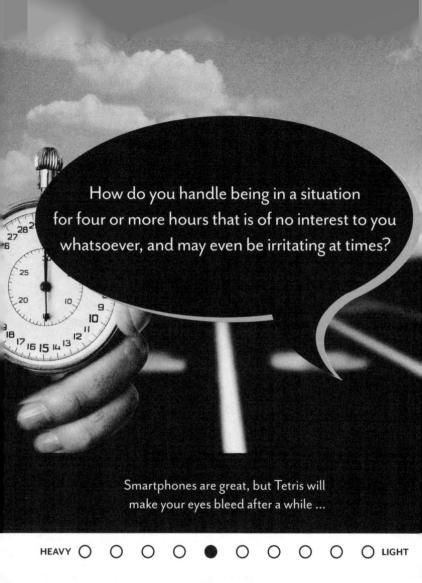

What one thing do at least five of your friends own that you do not care about?

Straight up. Not something you may be slightly jealous about, and are pretending not to care about. Because people know when you play that card.

HEAVY ○ ○ ○ ○ ○ ○ ○ ○ ○ ● LIGHT

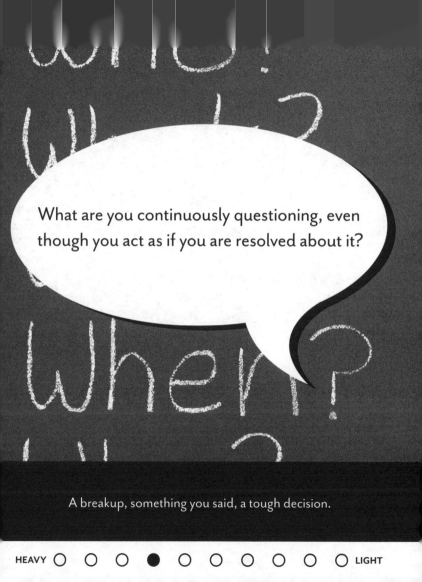

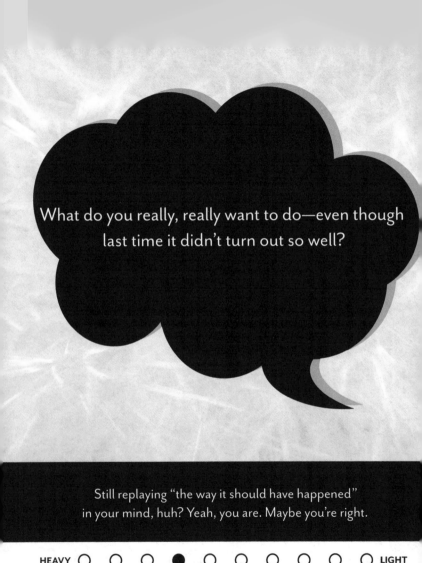

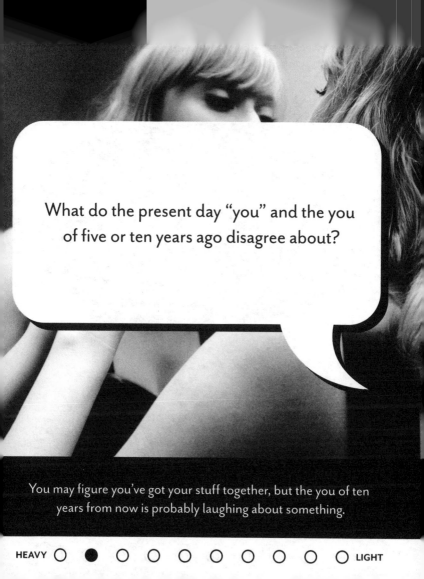

What do the present day "you" and the you of five or ten years ago disagree about?

You may figure you've got your stuff together, but the you of ten years from now is probably laughing about something.

HEAVY ○ ● ○ ○ ○ ○ ○ ○ ○ ○ LIGHT

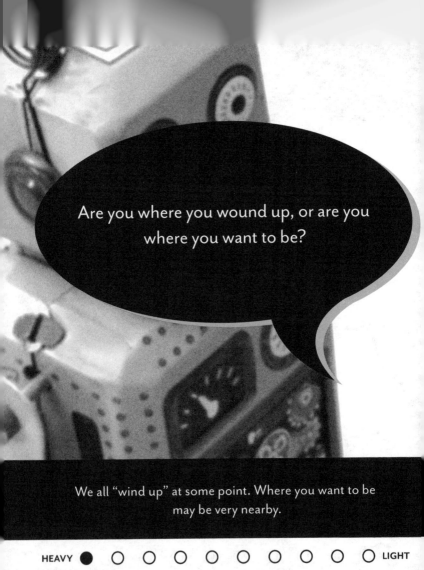

What did you talk yourself into thinking that you had changed, although nothing had actually changed?

Maybe you changed a little, for a while. Or maybe it didn't stick?

HEAVY ○ ● ○ ○ ○ ○ ○ ○ ○ ○ LIGHT

When did you reject advice that you later came to accept?

Maybe you didn't want to hear it yet.

HEAVY ○ ○ ● ○ ○ ○ ○ ○ ○ ○ LIGHT

What anecdote about you
seems like a story about a different person
when you hear it or think of it, because you know
that you are no longer "that way"?

It can be interesting to hear that story at first,
though after a while it may grow tiresome.

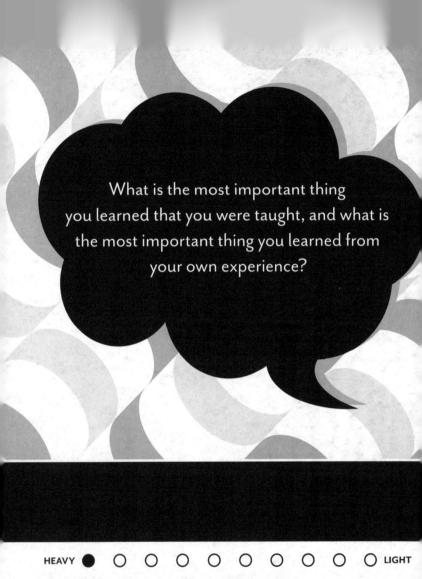

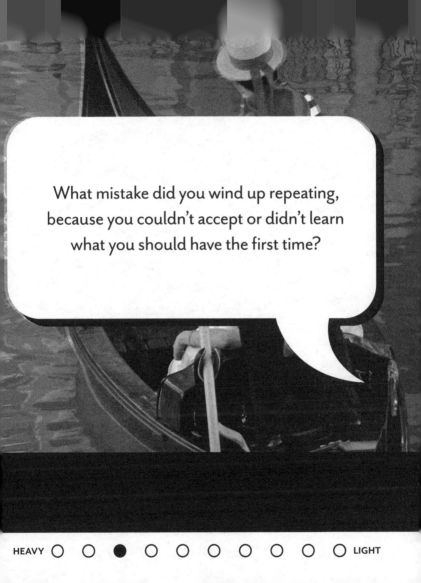

What mistake did you wind up repeating, because you couldn't accept or didn't learn what you should have the first time?

HEAVY ○ ○ ● ○ ○ ○ ○ ○ ○ ○ LIGHT

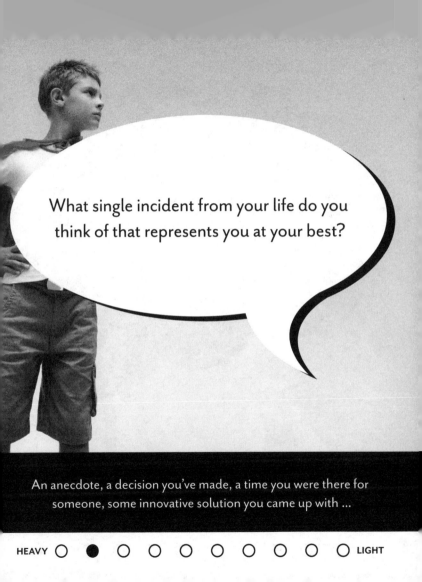

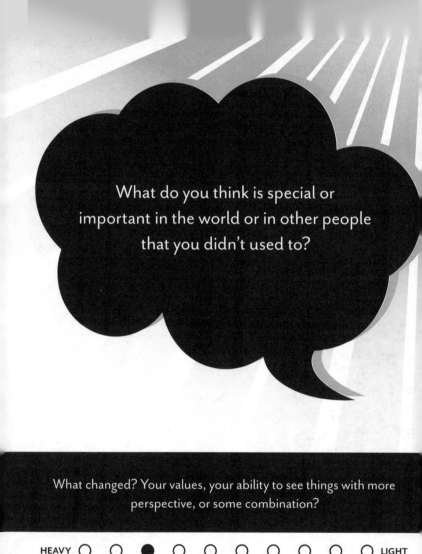

What do you think is special or important in the world or in other people that you didn't used to?

What changed? Your values, your ability to see things with more perspective, or some combination?

HEAVY ○ ○ ● ○ ○ ○ ○ ○ ○ ○ LIGHT

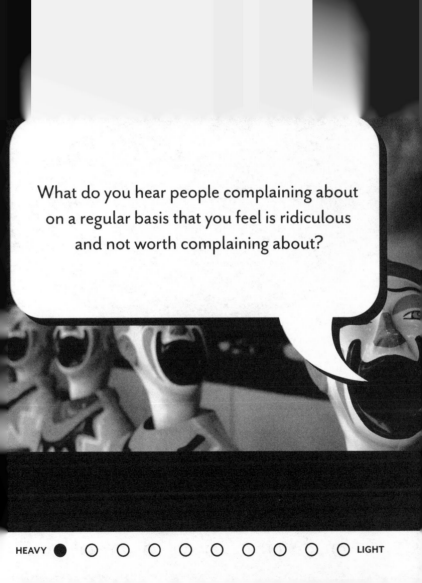

What did you do that you thought was going to cause some kind of huge problem, but instead nobody found out about it or nobody cared?

Maybe they should have, but you totally skated.

HEAVY   LIGHT

What are you glad that someone
stopped you from doing?

Were you definitely going to do it? Was the person that
stopped you a good friend or a casual acquaintance?

HEAVY ○ ○ ○ ● ○ ○ ○ ○ ○ ○ LIGHT

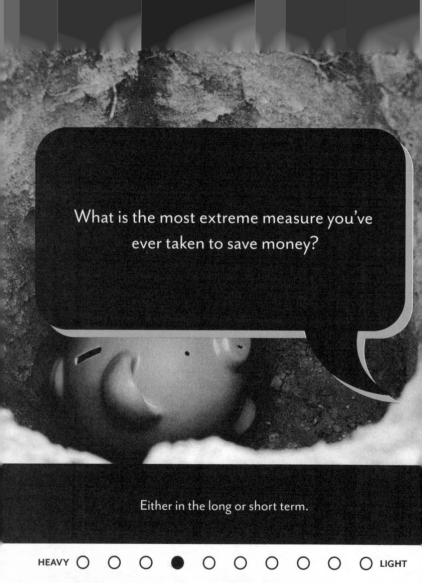

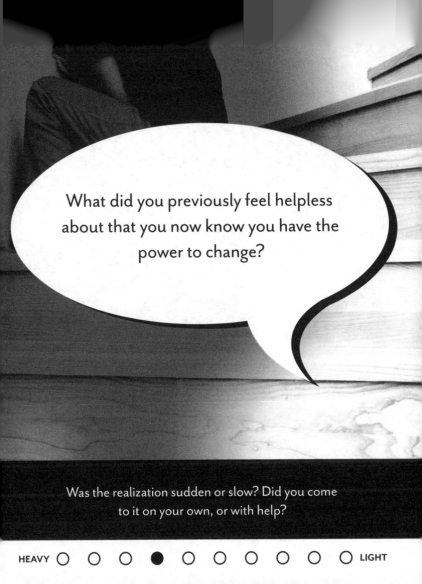

When were you shocked to discover you'd committed a "deal breaker" in a relationship?

People have rules that they don't realize are "rules." Sometimes, when you break one, you are very suddenly out the door.

HEAVY ○ ○ ● ○ ○ ○ ○ ○ ○ ○ LIGHT

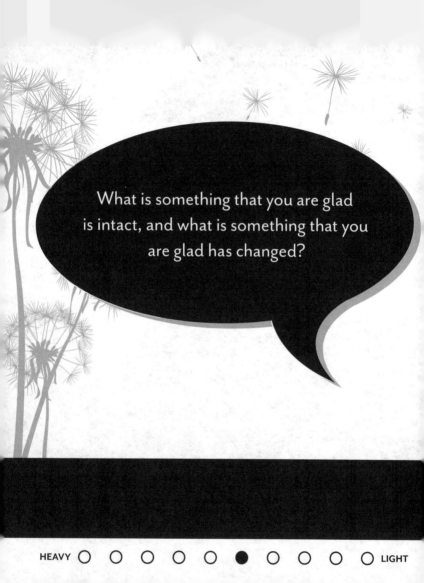

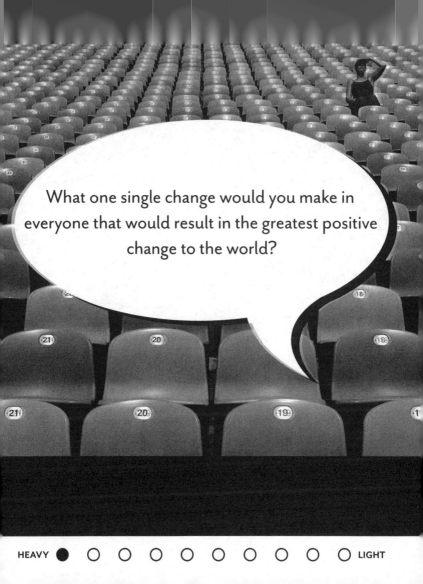

When did you most recently say,
"If I don't do this, I will always regret it?"
What was going on at the time?

Did you do it? Or did it need some planning? What's the status?
Yeah, we're in your face about this!

HEAVY ○ ○ ○ ○ ● ○ ○ ○ ○ ○ LIGHT

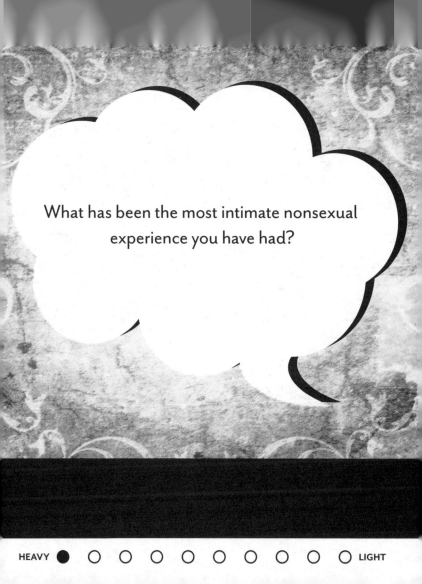

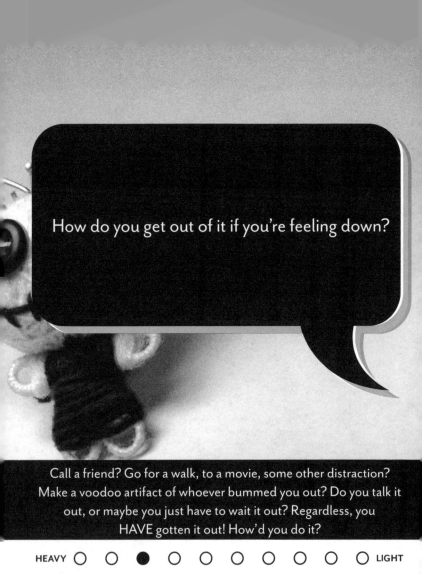

How do you get out of it if you're feeling down?

Call a friend? Go for a walk, to a movie, some other distraction? Make a voodoo artifact of whoever bummed you out? Do you talk it out, or maybe you just have to wait it out? Regardless, you HAVE gotten it out! How'd you do it?

HEAVY ○ ○ ● ○ ○ ○ ○ ○ ○ ○ LIGHT

What do you wish someone would say to you that no one has ever said to you?

Some acknowledgement? Some prodding?

What does everyone seem to accept that you find to be completely unacceptable?

Does this set you apart, or set you above?
You've got your reasons, let's hear them.

HEAVY   LIGHT

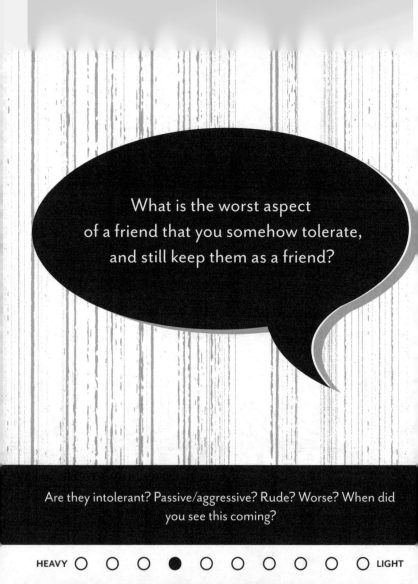

What change did you once hope for
that you are now GLAD did not happen?

What do you own that,
if someone else were to find it, they would
get the wrong impression of you?

Of course, it would also be revealing ... to an extent.

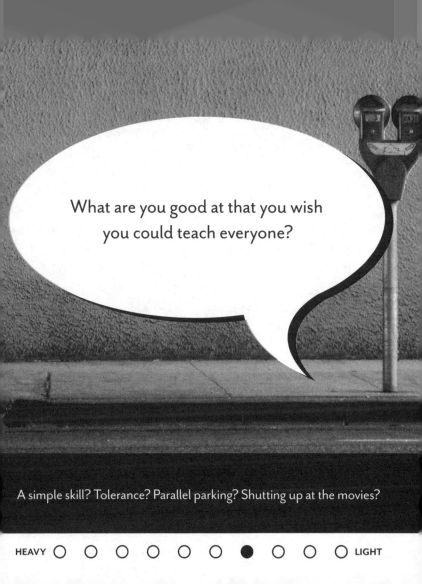

What is your favorite thing you've seen that you wish you had a picture of?

Describe. In detail.

HEAVY ○ ○ ● ○ ○ ○ ○ ○ ○ ○ LIGHT

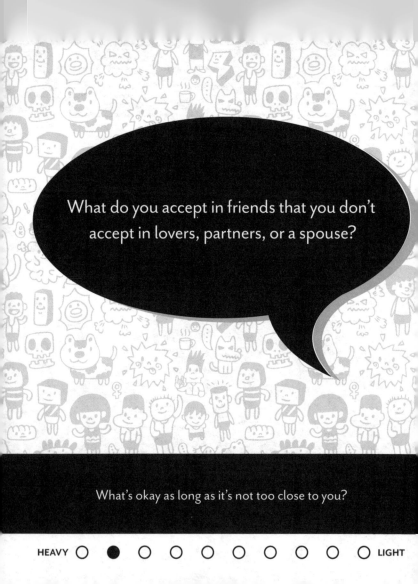

What do you accept in friends that you don't accept in lovers, partners, or a spouse?

What's okay as long as it's not too close to you?

HEAVY ○ ● ○ ○ ○ ○ ○ ○ ○ ○ LIGHT

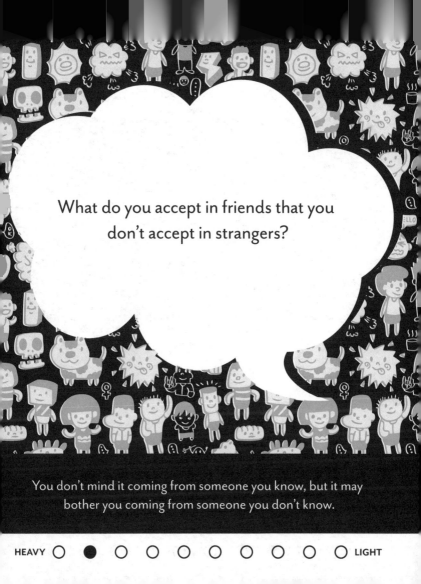

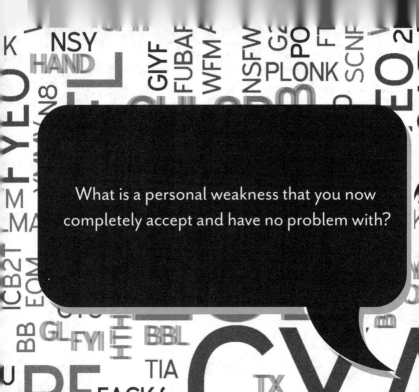

What is a personal weakness that you now completely accept and have no problem with?

Resolution. A good lesson to share.

HEAVY ○ ○ ● ○ ○ ○ ○ ○ ○ ○ LIGHT

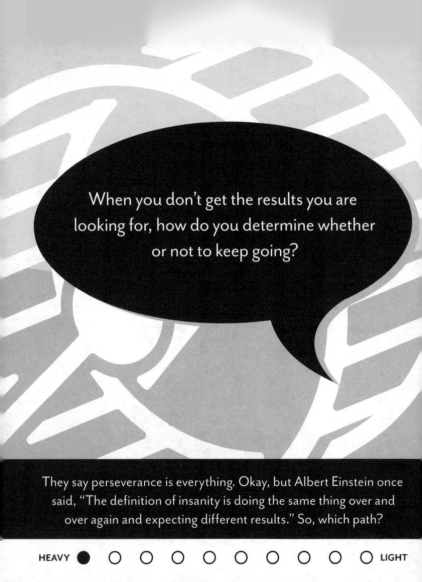

When did you first experience your intuition?

Tell the story. And, by the way, if you think
you haven't experienced it ... you have.

Who do you know that continues to shock or surprise you in a positive way, as if you were meeting them for the first time?

What have you wanted the most,
that you had to say "no" to?

A gift? A relationship? A little ... something?
Did you make the right decision?

HEAVY ○ ○ ● ○ ○ ○ ○ ○ ○ ○ LIGHT

Who do you have a "wordless" relationship with?

Where, when you see each other, you know exactly what's going on with each other, or what is on each other's mind, without anything being said.

HEAVY ○ ● ○ ○ ○ ○ ○ ○ ○ ○ LIGHT

How has your passion led you to act in some way that, you have to admit, is "crazy"?

Passion about a love, an artist, your convictions ...
is this like you? Is it not like you? Is this the new you?
Never saw that coming, huh? Speak on this.

HEAVY ● ○ ○ ○ ○ ○ ○ ○ ○ ○ LIGHT

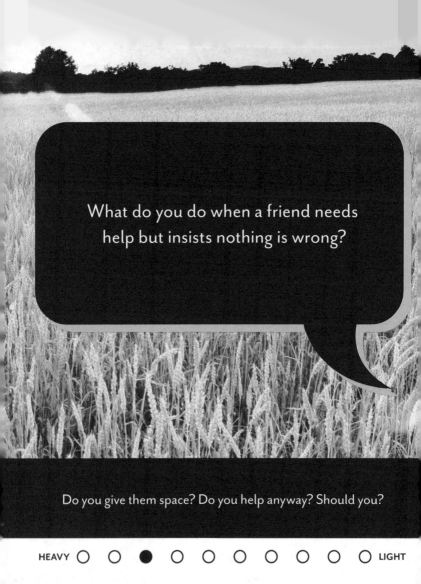

When did you react too severely because you hadn't heard the other side of the story?

Did loyalty lead you to judge too soon?
Were you too critical of someone close to you?

HEAVY ○ ○ ○ ● ○ ○ ○ ○ ○ ○ LIGHT

What conversation or action are you putting off?

As time goes on, is it more costly?

HEAVY ○ ○ ○ ○ ○ ○ ● ○ ○ ○ LIGHT

What's the last thing you heard or said on the condition of anonymity?

We won't tell ...

HEAVY ○ ○ ○ ○ ○ ○ ○ ○ ● ○ LIGHT

If you somehow found out in advance that the specific personal goals you have were not going to happen, what would you work on instead?

Goals take care of needs, but sometimes we make them too narrow. Get back in touch with the need and see what else you can do to take care of yourself.

HEAVY ○ ○ ● ○ ○ ○ ○ ○ ○ ○ LIGHT

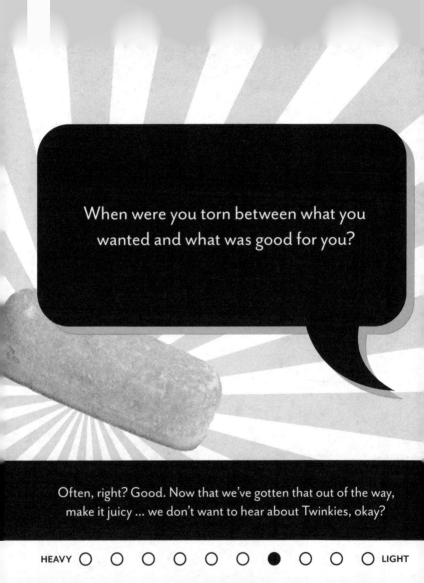

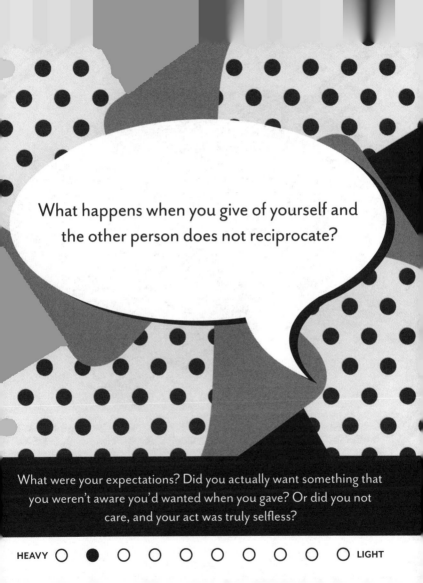

What happens when you give of yourself and the other person does not reciprocate?

What were your expectations? Did you actually want something that you weren't aware you'd wanted when you gave? Or did you not care, and your act was truly selfless?

HEAVY ○ ● ○ ○ ○ ○ ○ ○ ○ ○ LIGHT

At what point do you cut off patience?

It is necessary sometimes. Other times, being patient can be like waiting for a flight that got cancelled. At what point do you call it a day?

HEAVY ○ ● ○ ○ ○ ○ ○ ○ ○ ○ LIGHT

How honest are you when
you turn down an invitation?

"I like you, but not THAT much." "I love you, but I need extra
patience and energy to deal with your B.S., which I don't have at
the moment." "I can't pretend to like your band anymore."
How far do you go?

HEAVY ○ ○ ○ ○ ○ ● ○ ○ ○ ○ LIGHT

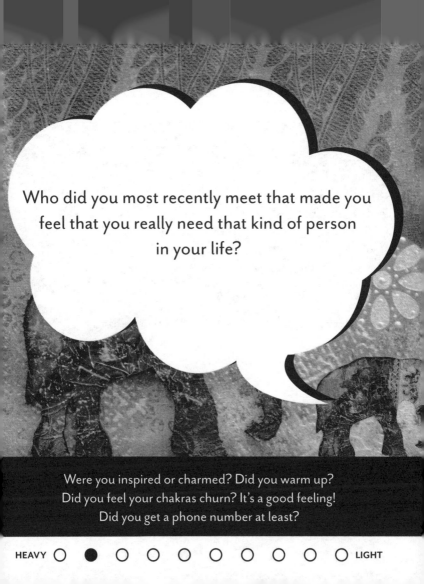

What are people expecting of you?

Are they waiting for you to produce? To fess up? To show up? To give it all you've got? To inspire and deliver at the same time?

HEAVY ○ ○ ○ ○ ○ ● ○ ○ ○ ○ LIGHT

The last time you got good or great news, who did you tell first?

Did you get the reaction you were looking for?
Hopefully, they know you were honoring them.

HEAVY   LIGHT

What are you still counting on that has not happened so far?

Are you waiting to hear from someone?
Is there a great event you want to occur?

HEAVY ○ ○ ○ ○ ● ○ ○ ○ ○ ○ LIGHT

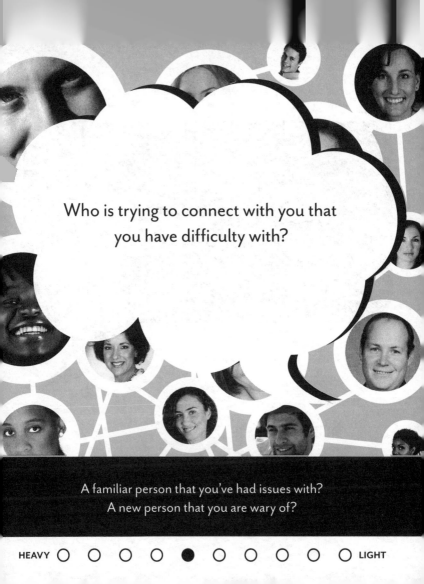

When you hear that something involves risk, how does that affect your ability to go forward?

You want something different. That's why the word risk came up. The thing that we call "safety" may actually be riskier than risk. It's just more of the same.

HEAVY ⚪ ⚫ ⚪ ⚪ ⚪ ⚪ ⚪ ⚪ ⚪ ⚪ LIGHT

If you need to communicate to a friend,
and talking doesn't work,
are you willing to take additional steps?

Like? Getting other people in on it, yelling, parking
an obtrusive object in their driveway. Depends on what's at
stake. Otherwise, face the fact that the issue or the friendship
itself may in fact be optional ...

HEAVY ○ ○ ○ ● ○ ○ ○ ○ ○ ○ LIGHT

What ticks people off that doesn't
seem to bother you at all?

HEAVY ○ ○ ○ ○ ○ ● ○ ○ ○ ○ ○ LIGHT

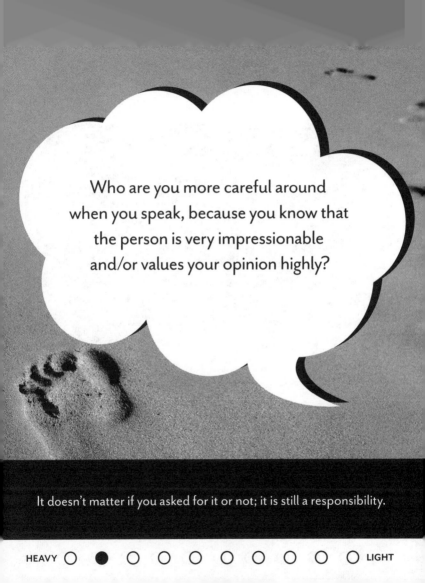

Who are you more careful around when you speak, because you know that the person is very impressionable and/or values your opinion highly?

It doesn't matter if you asked for it or not; it is still a responsibility.

HEAVY ○ ● ○ ○ ○ ○ ○ ○ ○ ○ ○ LIGHT

What have you learned from an artist or someone in the arts that is of equal value to something you've learned from someone you know?

It is said that art exists to help us access feelings we may normally be unable to. What has your experience been?

HEAVY ○ ● ○ ○ ○ ○ ○ ○ ○ ○ LIGHT

What do you want to give a friend
that they are not ready for?

Specific advice? A possession of theirs? A difficult truth? MORE
of your friendship? Great amounts of love?

Who is holding back with you?

Are you feeling that from someone? Do they love you, but cannot say so? Is there some big truth they have that they aren't sure you'll be cool with, or are up to dealing with?

HEAVY ○ ○ ○ ● ○ ○ ○ ○ ○ ○ LIGHT

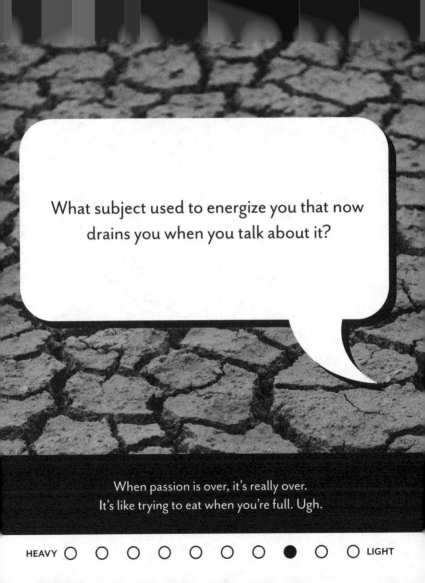

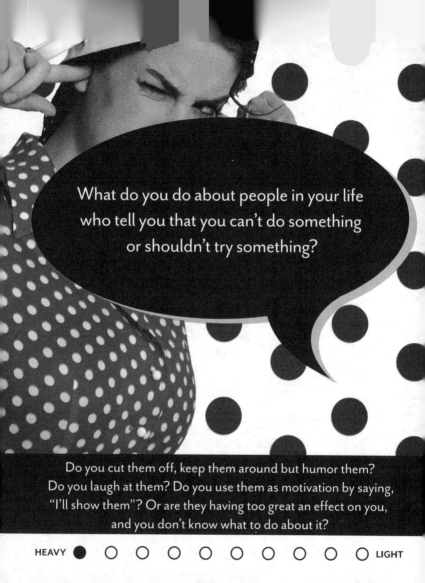

Who haven't you thought about
in a long time that you used to think about
to the point of distraction?

Could be a past love, a love that never was, a crush,
a famous person. After all of that attention, how did you come
to the point of not thinking about them at all?

HEAVY ○ ○ ● ○ ○ ○ ○ ○ ○ ○ LIGHT

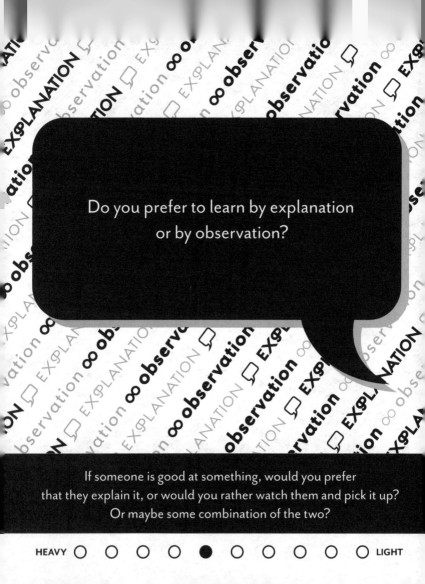

Do you prefer to learn by explanation
or by observation?

If someone is good at something, would you prefer
that they explain it, or would you rather watch them and pick it up?
Or maybe some combination of the two?

HEAVY ○ ○ ○ ○ ● ○ ○ ○ ○ ○ LIGHT

What popular artist, trend or gadget is actually underrated because of its popularity?

Everyone is so busy being irritated by its presence
that they forget (or ignore) that there is actually quality there.
Tough break, curmudgeon! Fess up.

HEAVY ○ ○ ○ ○ ○ ○ ○ ○ ○ ● LIGHT

What strong opinion or passion that you shared with a friend does one of you no longer have?

Did it anchor the friendship? Did your friendship change or was that bond just a starting point?

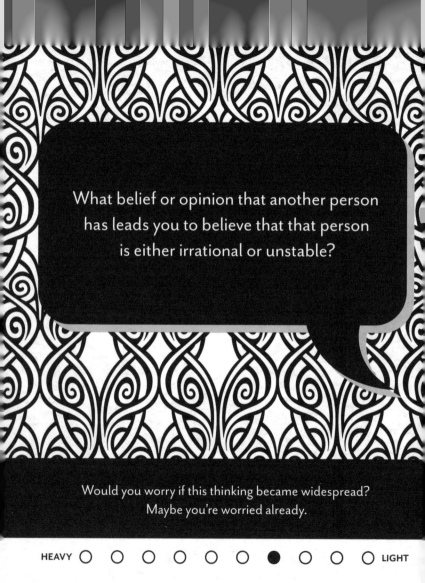

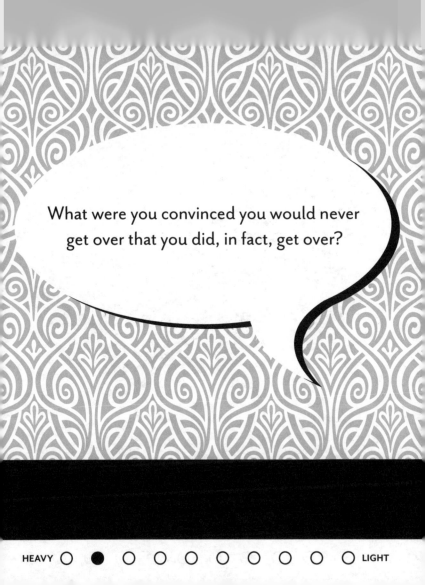

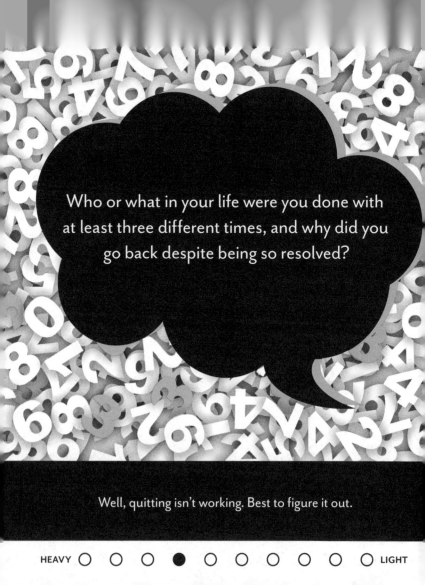

Who or what in your life were you done with at least three different times, and why did you go back despite being so resolved?

Well, quitting isn't working. Best to figure it out.

HEAVY ○ ○ ○ ● ○ ○ ○ ○ ○ ○ LIGHT

What gift have you received that you have made the most use of?

A practical gift? A gift from the heart?

HEAVY ○ ○ ○ ○ ● ○ ○ ○ ○ ○ LIGHT

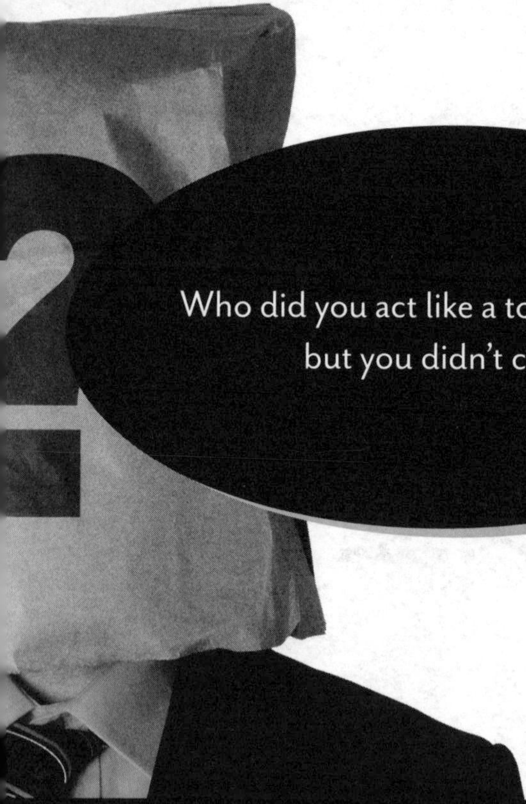

Who did you act like a total fool over, but you didn't care?

Something real good must have been going on ...

HEAVY ○ ● ○ ○ ○ ○ ○ ○ ○ ○ LIGHT

When you meet people, what do you think they know about you even without your having said anything about it?

Do you come off with a certain vibe? Do you think people can know something you've been through without any mention of it?

HEAVY ○ ○ ○ ○ ○ ○ ● ○ ○ ○ LIGHT

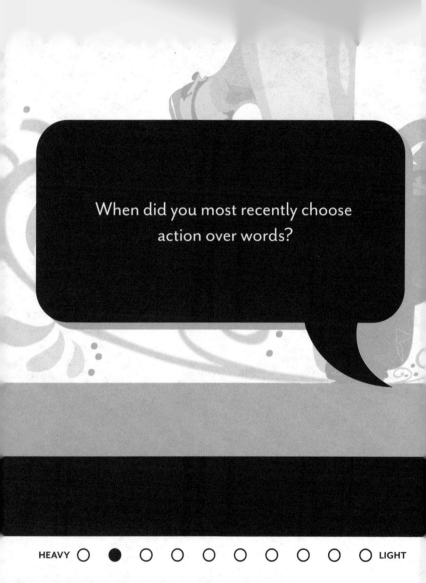

When did you most recently choose
action over words?

HEAVY ○ ● ○ ○ ○ ○ ○ ○ ○ ○ LIGHT

Are you immediately accessible, or do you tend to reveal yourself over time?

HEAVY ○ ○ ○ ○ ● ○ ○ ○ ○ LIGHT

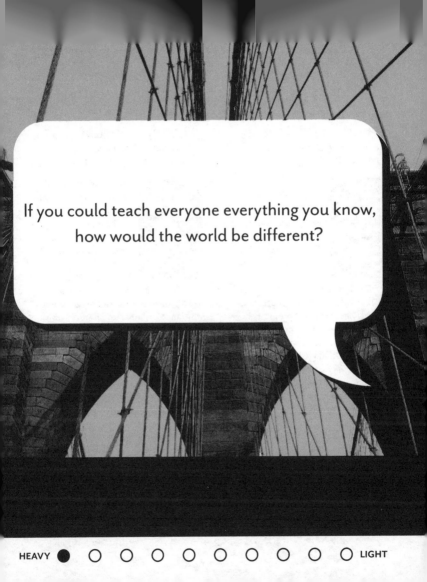

If you could teach everyone everything you know, how would the world be different?

HEAVY ● ○ ○ ○ ○ ○ ○ ○ ○ ○ LIGHT